An OPUS Book

Modern

Ann Waswo is Lecturer in Modern Japanese History at the University of Oxford, a member of the Nissan Institute of Japanese Studies, and a fellow of St Antony's College, Oxford.

OPUS General Editors

Christopher Butler
Robert Evans
John Skorupski

OPUS books provide concise, original, and authoritative introductions to a wide range of subjects in the humanities and sciences. They are written by experts for the general reader as well as for students.

Modern Japanese Society

1868–1994

Ann Waswo

Oxford   New York
OXFORD UNIVERSITY PRESS
1996

Oxford University Press, Walton Street, Oxford OX2 6DP

Oxford New York
Athens Auckland Bangkok Bombay
Calcutta Cape Town Dar es Salaam Delhi
Florence Hong Kong Istanbul Karachi
Kuala Lumpur Madras Madrid Melbourne
Mexico City Nairobi Paris Singapore
Taipei Tokyo Toronto
and associated companies in
Berlin Ibadan

Oxford is a trade mark of Oxford University Press

© Ann Waswo 1996

First published as an Oxford University Press paperback 1996

All rights reserved. No part of this publication may be reproduced, stored in a retrieval system, or transmitted, in any form or by any means, without the prior permission in writing of Oxford University Press. Within the UK, exceptions are allowed in respect of any fair dealing for the purpose of research or private study, or criticism or review, as permitted under the Copyright, Designs and Patents Act, 1988, or in the case of reprographic reproduction in accordance with the terms of the licences issued by the Copyright Licensing Agency. Enquiries concerning reproduction outside these terms and in other countries should be sent to the Rights Department, Oxford University Press, at the address above

This book is sold subject to the condition that it shall not, by way of trade or otherwise, be lent, re-sold, hired out or otherwise circulated without the publisher's prior consent in any form of binding or cover other than that in which it is published and without a similar condition including this condition being imposed on the subsequent purchaser

British Library Cataloguing in Publication Data
Data available

Library of Congress Cataloging in Publication Data
Waswo, Ann.
 Modern Japanese society, 1868–1994 / Ann Waswo.
   p.   cm.
 "OPUS book."
 Includes bibliographical references and index.
 1. Japan—History—1868–   I. Title.
DS881.9.W383 1996 952.03—dc20   95-31534
ISBN 0-19-289228-2

10 9 8 7 6 5 4 3 2 1

Typeset by Pure Tech India Ltd., Pondicherry
Printed in Great Britain
by Mackays
Chatham, Kent

Contents

List of Figures   vi
List of Tables   vi
Map of Japan and Eastern Asia   viii

Introduction   1
1 On the Meiji Restoration   8
2 Creating the New Nation   22
3 Toward an Industrial Economy   35
4 Protest from Below   54
5 The Military in Politics   76
6 Modernization and its Discontents   90
7 The Postwar 'Economic Miracle' and its Consequences   104
8 Japanese Society in the Early 1990s   127

Notes   164
Select Bibliography   169
Index   177

List of Figures

1. Geographical concentration of tenancy disputes, 1917–1930   70
2. Japanese discourse about modernization   92

List of Tables

1. Population by place of residence, 1950–1990   130
2. Labor force by sector and employment status, 1950–1990   131
3. Age distribution, 1950–2010   133

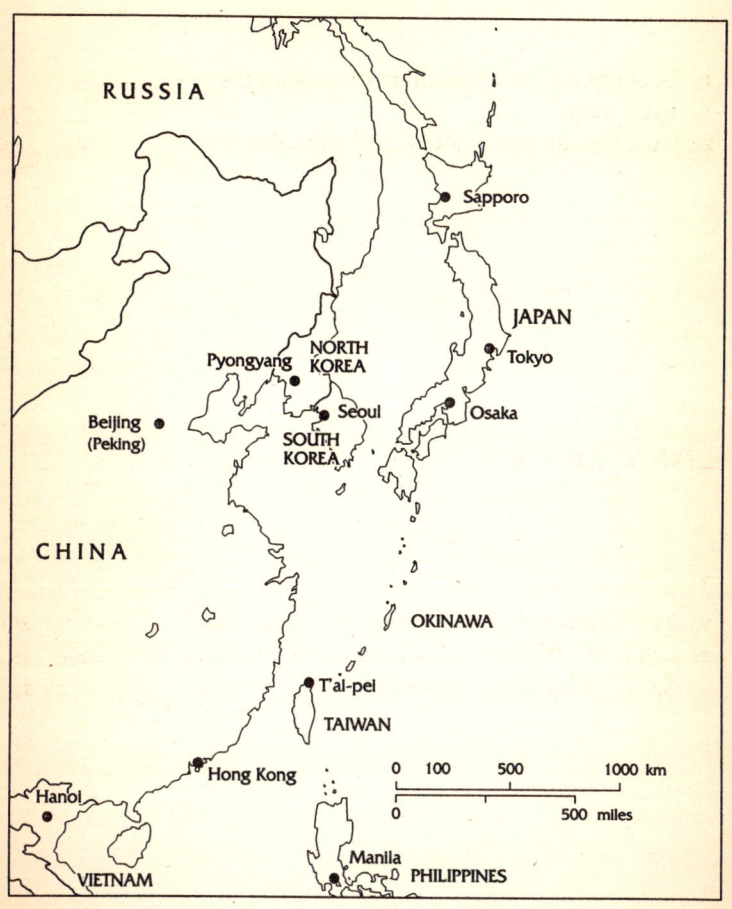

Map of Japan and Eastern Asia

Introduction

About 125 years ago, in the early 1870s, Japan was what we might now term a 'third world' or 'developing' country. A fledgling central government, dating from the Meiji Restoration of 1868, exercised only limited control over the population and resources of the Japanese archipelago. The economy was overwhelmingly agrarian, with some 80 per cent of the labor force in farming and some 70 per cent of gross national product deriving from food production and food processing. A classic 'third world' pattern prevailed in the country's foreign trade, with exports consisting largely of primary products from the land and imports of manufactured goods from the industrialized and industrializing countries of the West.

Nor was trade the only way in which the West impinged on Japan at this time. The newly unified island nation also found itself confronted by the West's system of international law, which differed markedly from the system of inter-state relations practiced for centuries by Japan's great continental neighbor China, and by the West's 'diplomacy of imperialism', for which East Asia as a whole—like Africa—was a major arena in the late nineteenth century. Not yet entirely secure from challenge at home, the new Meiji government of Japan was also a weak force in the region, much more an observer of events that might well shape the region's future than a participant in them.

By about 1914, Japan had become what we might now term a 'newly industrializing country' (NIC). The central government had long since gained full and effective control over the entire country, and had begun to manifest some of the authoritarian tendencies associated with many NICs of more recent vintage. Although the economy and society remained predominantly agrarian, a nascent industrial sector was expanding at the rate of some 6 per cent per year on average, and Japan's trading position had shifted in significant ways. Exports of domestically produced light manufactured goods, most notably of cotton textiles, were increasing, as were imports of machinery to enable Japan to produce such capital-intensive goods as locomotives for the domestic railway network in future. Not insignificantly, Japan had moved from observer to participant status in the diplomacy of imperialism within East Asia and now possessed a formal empire of its own, consisting chiefly of Taiwan (as of 1895) and Korea (as of 1910).

Today, roughly fifty years after its defeat in 1945 in the Second World War, Japan is an economic giant, whose gross national product per capita exceeds that of the United States of America. Its trading position is of the classic 'first world' type: exports of manufactured goods and technology, imports of raw materials and food. Less than 7 per cent of the labor force is engaged in agriculture; the overwhelming majority work in the secondary and tertiary sectors of the economy, and most of the Japanese people live in cities. Their country is the only non-Western member of the élite Group of Seven nations within the Organization for Economic Cooperation and Development (OECD), and their government has begun lobbying for permanent membership of the Security Council of the United Nations.

In the pages that follow I will examine selected facets of the social history of Japan during this eventful period. Let me emphasize the word 'selected'. This is not a comprehensive social history of modern Japan, much less a survey of Japan's modern history as a whole. My purpose has been far more limited: to provide a reasonably coherent discussion of topics and issues which have been relegated to the sidelines in much of the Western literature on Japan to date.

The eight chapters into which this book is divided originated in whole or in part as lectures I have given in recent years to undergraduate students of history at the University of Oxford, as background and supplementation to the reading, thinking, and writing they have done for weekly tutorials on such 'mainstream' topics as Japanese imperialism, party politics in the 1920s, the Manchurian Incident of 1931, and the reforms of the Occupation era, 1945–52. The chapters are loosely linked by chronology, but also by three related themes.

First and foremost is the role of 'ordinary' Japanese in the unfolding history of their country. Until fairly recently, much of what has been written about modern Japan in the West has focused on political and economic élites and on the 'great events'—some of them seen as illustrious, others as ignominious—in which those élites figured. While it cannot be denied that the behavior of Japanese élites over the past century or so has given historians of this persuasion plenty of grist for their mills, it must also be acknowledged that the end result has been only a partial, and at times a highly misleading, explication of Japan's historical experience. It is not simply that the common man and woman have been ignored. Both have been portrayed, implicitly as well as explicitly, as passive and docile beings who would do as, and only as, their superiors commanded. I will attempt to demonstrate that this has not generally been the case.

Second, and following from the above, I will attempt to delineate the relationship between the state and the people since the late nineteenth century. This relationship has been considerably more complicated, I think, than much of the élite-centered literature would indicate and brings us to one of the major continuities of modern Japanese history: a state bureaucracy which has always sought to monitor and manage Japanese society, and has done so with considerable skill. Less oppressive and unresponsive to popular grievances under the Imperial Japanese Constitution (1889–1947) and also less monolithic than some accounts would have us believe, the bureaucracy was only modestly affected by the reforms of the post-Second World War Occupation and has continued to try to keep one step ahead of the Japanese people, anticipating their discontents and seeking to attend to at least some of them.

To assert this continuity is not to deny important changes in the distribution of political power within Japan since the end of the Occupation in 1952. The people, in whom now resides the sovereignty once vested in emperors, enjoy considerably greater civil liberties under the current, American-inspired constitution than under the old. The party politicians whom they elect to the national Diet and the cabinets formed by the majority party (or, as of 1993 and perhaps for a while thereafter, majority coalition) in its lower house have had and continue to develop a far greater say in the determination of national policy than used to be the case. Various interest groups exist and compete—legally as well as illegally—for influence over legislation and public policy. In comparison with the realities of politics and political systems elsewhere in the world, Japan has clearly become a functioning democracy, but it is, I think, a highly technocratic democracy in which bureaucratic experts, selected as they have been since the establishment of a civil-service system in the 1890s on the basis of generally accepted evidence of merit, possess considerable authority and leverage.

Third, I will attempt to show that there are historical explanations—by which I mean explanations based on trends, events, and the real or perceived problems of the moment—for many of the features of modern Japanese history and modern Japanese society that have been attributed rather too easily by some to Japan's 'unique' and 'enduring' cultural traditions. Of course, Japan today possesses a distinctive culture, but that culture has been and remains no more static than in other countries. Traditions have been invented and reinvented on numerous occasions in the past. Norms and values, as well as behavior, have changed in subtle and not-so-subtle ways. Recurrent assertions of the 'uniqueness' of Japanese culture over the past century or so, stemming primarily from within the Japanese political and economic establishment, are themselves historical phenomena that merit examination.

I assume little or no previous knowledge of Japan past or present on the part of readers, and for that reason I have tried to keep Japanese terminology—and, less defensibly, Japanese names—to a minimum. Nor will it be necessary for readers to bone up on contemporary semiotic or other theories, for what follows is a fairly conventional, descriptive treatment of the subject. That there are gaps in the coverage I freely acknowledge, as I do my reliance on the published work of other scholars for much of what I do include. With a few exceptions, only direct quotations and references to topics beyond the chronological or conceptual limits I have imposed are footnoted in the text, but for each chapter I have provided a list of important readings. Only books and articles available in English are included in the latter, but this is in no way intended to slight the contributions of Japanese scholars, on whom all of us in Japanese Studies in the West depend.

Finally, I should make some observations about the span of time with which this book is concerned. I begin with the Meiji Restoration of 1868 and end with the early 1990s, but the intervening century and a quarter only approximates the 'modern' period in Japanese history. The former date is merely one of two conventional starting-points, the other being the arrival of Commodore Perry's naval squadron in 1853 and the opening of Japan after more than two centuries of self-imposed isolation, and I transgress both mid-nineteenth-century boundaries—as do other scholars—to discuss the preceding Tokugawa period, not merely as background but as a source of many 'modern' or 'protomodern' phenomena.

The latter date is also problematic. Granted, one can identify a cluster of major events in the early 1990s—the bursting of the highly speculative 'bubble economy' of the late 1980s and the onset of severe recession; the passage of controversial enabling legislation and the participation of Japanese personnel in UN peacekeeping operations in Cambodia; the defeat of the Liberal Democratic Party, the governing party of Japan without interruption since 1955, and the intense political infighting and shifting party affiliations that ensued—but whether these and other events one might cite constitute the end of an era or not is debatable. Even if they do, it is debatable whether they mark the end of Japan's 'modern' era. To some observers, that occurred earlier, in the 1970s and early 1980s, as Japan first reached 'post-industrial' status and then entered or began to experience 'post-modernity'. These intriguing questions I leave to others. I have continued the discussion to the early 1990s simply because I figured, with no little encouragement from my editors, that most of the intended readers of this book, especially the younger among them, would have regarded an earlier stopping-point as unsatisfactory.

The past does not automatically dissolve into phases or eras, nor does the present necessarily represent an improvement over what has gone before. To divide time is to interpret it, and in most of the literature on Japan scholars have used great events to divide modern Japanese history into 'meaningful' segments. The crudest division, in my opinion, centers exclusively on the Second World War, consigning virtually everything that occurred after 1853 or 1868 to 'prewar' Japan and everything that occurred after 1945 to 'postwar' Japan. Only slightly less crude, in that it does not consign the war to inevitability or immutable significance, is division by imperial reign, or *nengō*, of which there have been four since the Restoration: the Meiji (1868–1912), Taishō (1912–26), Shōwa (1926–89), and Heisei (1989–) eras.

At present, historians both in Japan and in the West are grappling with the periodization, and paradigms, they have inherited from their predecessors, finding new continuities and discontinuities apace in Japan's modern 'trajectory'. Although I do not regard that trajectory as a seamless whole, I have imposed no explicit periodization on the century and a quarter of social history under review. The sketch of Japan's transformation presented at the outset of this introduction should be regarded as nothing more than a device to illustrate some of the changes that have occurred in Japan since the nineteenth century to those unfamiliar with Japan's past.

Chapter 6 has previously appeared in print as 'Modernization and Cultural Identity' in *Asian Affairs* (Feb. 1988), and thanks are due to the Royal Society for Asian Affairs for permitting its republication, in somewhat altered form, here. Thanks are also due to the students I have taught over the years in both the United States and the United Kingdom, whose questions and observations have helped shape my own thinking about the social history of Japan, and to Jenny Corbett, Roger Goodman, Mark Rebick, and Arthur Stockwin, colleagues at the Nissan Institute of Japanese Studies, Oxford, for their helpful criticisms of portions of a manuscript that has taken far longer than I anticipated to complete. It should go without saying that I alone am responsible for errors and other shortcomings in the end result.

1

On the Meiji Restoration

*T*okugawa Yoshinobu, the fifteenth Tokugawa shogun, submitted his resignation to the emperor in November 1867, bringing to an end over two centuries and a half of *de facto* rule of Japan by the Tokugawa house. In January 1868 the restoration of rule by the emperor was proclaimed, and by 1869 all forces loyal to the Tokugawa had been defeated. In the latter year the young emperor Mutsuhito, to be known by the reign name of Meiji, proceeded from Kyoto to Edo (now renamed Tokyo, or eastern capital) and moved into the shogun's castle.

In the Charter Oath issued in the emperor's name in April 1868 it was proclaimed that:

1. An assembly shall be widely convoked, and all measures shall be decided by open discussion.
2. High and low shall be of one mind, and the national economy and finances shall be greatly strengthened.
3. All civil and military officials together, and the common people as well, shall all achieve their aspirations, and thus the people's minds shall not be made weary.
4. Evil practices of the past shall be abandoned, and actions shall be based on international usage.
5. Knowledge shall be sought all over the world, and the foundations of Imperial rule shall be strengthened.[1]

Soon the fledgling imperial government was to announce a series of bold initiatives: the centralization of political authority in a unified nation state, the industrialization of the economy, the formal legal and social equality of all the emperor's subjects, universal male conscription, and the creation of a nationwide education system so that 'there shall, in the future, be no community with an illiterate family, nor a family with an illiterate person'.[2]

To many Western observers at the time, the events known as the Meiji Restoration represented the reawakening of Japan after centuries of feudal torpor. They had no doubt that the key role in that reawakening had been played by the West—by Commodore Perry, who had arrived in Uraga Bay with his squadron of four ships in 1853 and demanded that Japan end its self-imposed isolation, by the diplomats who had negotiated the first commercial treaties with Japan a few years later, and, last but not least, by the undeniable superiority of Western ideas and institutions. The Tokugawa shogunate had '[given] way to the irresistible momentum of a higher civilization'.[3]

In reality, the Restoration was not at all that simple. To be sure, the West had played an important role in bringing the events of 1868 about, but more as catalyst than cause. The roots of the Restoration lay deeper, in developments within Japan itself during the long period of Tokugawa ascendancy.

A full understanding of the Restoration, then, requires detailed examination of Japan's pre-Restoration past, and that simply is not possible here. Instead, I propose to provide a forward-looking discussion of the Restoration, aimed primarily at laying a foundation for the analysis of developments in Japanese society *after* 1868. What were the major features of the *ancien régime* that was cast aside in 1867/8? Who did the casting aside, and why?

The Ancien Régime

The ascendancy of the Tokugawa house from 1603, when Tokugawa Ieyasu acquired the title of shogun, to 1867, when Tokugawa Yoshinobu surrendered it, marked the culmination of centuries of progressively greater control over Japan by members of the warrior (*bushi*) class. At the apex of the regime was the shogun. He and his direct retainers between them controlled about one-quarter of the land area of Japan, including its major cities and its precious metal mines. The shogun also controlled Japan's relations with other countries.

Next were some 260 great lords, or daimyo, each of whom swore an oath of allegiance to the shogun, the overlord, on succeeding to the headship of his house. In return, he received confirmation of his possession of a given domain, or fief. Within his domain, the daimyo enjoyed a considerable degree of autonomy, with powers to collect taxes (principally on agricultural output), regulate commerce, and dispense justice.

Both the shogun and the daimyo possessed their own retainers, or samurai, who carried out civil and military duties within their respective territories. The retainer band in any one domain was itself a hierarchy. Those at its top were entitled by their rank to occupy the highest offices in the domain; they maintained large households, with many servants, and also had numerous retainers of their own. Next came the ordinary samurai, who filled the middle range of domain offices. Lower samurai, the many retainers at the bottom of the hierarchy, had access to correspondingly low-ranking offices (e.g. as messengers, gatekeepers, or fish-buyers in their daimyo's kitchen) and, at best, might have kept one or two household servants. Far more numerous than the knights of medieval England, the samurai, together with their families, probably comprised some 6–7 per cent of the total population of Japan.

The Tokugawa had achieved their hegemonic position in 1603 by means of victories in a series of battles that brought to an end over a century of intermittent warfare among rival military houses and coalitions of daimyo. It was during this long period of warfare (the setting, it might be mentioned, for Akira Kurosawa's impressive cinematic translations of *Macbeth* and *King Lear*) that conditions in Japan most closely resembled those of high feudalism in Europe. It was also during this period that virtually all vestiges of an earlier, Chinese-inspired system of imperial rule over the country came to an end. Only the emperors and the court aristocracy remained; cut off as they were from the estates on whose revenues they had once depended, they lived a much-reduced existence.

It is said that one sixteenth-century emperor lay unburied for months, owing to lack of funds for an appropriate funeral. Another made ends meet by selling his calligraphy in the streets of Kyoto, the imperial capital. Goyōzei, the emperor at the time of Tokugawa Ieyasu's final victory at the great battle of Sekigahara in 1600, was not in a position to deny Ieyasu the title of shogun (an abbreviation of *sei-i taishōgun*, or barbarian-quelling generalissimo). Until 1867, his successors continued to confer that title on each new head of the Tokugawa house, thereby recognizing him as their military deputy and *de facto* ruler of Japan. In return, the emperors received respectful treatment and a comfortable annual sum from the revenue on lands set aside by the shogunate for the maintenance of the imperial court and the performance of important religious observances.

Having achieved hegemony, and a legitimizing title from the emperor, Ieyasu began the process of consolidating his position. Of the various measures he and his immediate successors implemented to prevent renewed warfare or any other challenge to the new shogunate, four merit our attention here.

First was the policy of national seclusion, or *sakoku*. European missionaries and traders had been active in Japan since the mid-sixteenth century, and their presence was viewed with mixed feelings by the new shogunate. Continued contact with the Europeans, and with the Chinese and Koreans, was acceptable if and only if the shogunate benefited to a far greater extent than any of its former or potential rivals. When attempts to develop Edo as a port for foreign trade failed, the shogunate took steps to secure monopoly control over existing trade elsewhere in the country. At roughly the same time, in the aftermath of an armed revolt with Christian overtones in northern Kyushu, the shogunate cracked down on Christianity.

By 1641 all Europeans except the Dutch had been expelled from Japan, and both the Dutch and the Chinese were confined to special trading quarters in Nagasaki, a city under direct shogunal control. No Japanese was allowed to leave the country, nor could any Japanese then abroad return home. Christianity was declared illegal, and all Japanese were forced to register at

Buddhist temples. Those Japanese Christians who would not renounce their faith were executed, as were a number of European missionaries who refused to leave the country.

To those Western observers mentioned earlier who saw the return of the West to Japanese shores as the primary cause of the Meiji Restoration, it was taken as given that national seclusion had been a disaster for Japan. Deprived of the stimulus of unrestricted foreign trade and of free contact with Europe during the scientific and industrial revolutions, they reckoned, the country must have stagnated economically and culturally for over 200 years. Subsequent empirical research has shown, however, that this was not the case. By preventing further contact between the daimyo and foreigners, and terminating a rather brisk trade in European weapons, the policy of national seclusion eliminated a potent source of further conflict, and it may have saved one or more Japanese islands from colonization. During the long *Pax Tokugawa* that resulted—generation after generation of domestic tranquility, except for the occasional highly localized disturbance—considerable economic and cultural development could and did occur.

The second measure to note was the system of alternate attendance, or *sankin kōtai*, which required the daimyo to spend a period of time—usually every other year—in residence in Edo, the shogun's capital. When they returned to their domains, they were compelled to leave their wives and heirs behind as hostages to their good behavior. That the need to maintain two suitable residences, one in their domains and one in Edo, and to travel in procession between the two, imposed a financial burden on the daimyo was seen by shogunal officials as a further advantage of the system, since what the daimyo spent on 'butter' they could not spend on 'guns'.

Clearly designed as a means of controlling the daimyo and preserving the peace, the system of alternate attendance had some further, longer term, and largely unforeseen consequences that deserve at least brief mention. The recurrent presence of the daimyo, after the shogun the most powerful and wealthiest men in Japan, and the continual residence of their families served as a magnet for merchants and artisans, who flocked to Edo to cater to their needs, as well as to those of the shogunate itself. By 1800 the city had a population of over one million, making it one of the largest cities in the world at the time. Road and sea transport in the immediate region of Edo and then beyond into the hinterland was improved to serve the material needs of the city and to facilitate the journeys of the daimyo to and from it. In Edo the daimyo, although barred from any formal role in shogunal policymaking, had ample opportunities for informal communication with shogunal officials and among themselves. On their periodic return trips to their domains they, and their many retainers, took with them the new fashions and entertainments for which Edo increasingly became famous, a first step in the diffusion of those fashions and entertainments to the provinces and in the creation, despite political decentralization, of a national culture.

All daimyo were induced to convert a share of the tax revenue they received in rice and other commodities from the commoners in their domains into cash to finance their processions to and from Edo and their establishments in the capital, thereby contributing to the commercialization of the economy and the growth of the city of Osaka as a major center for trade and transshipment. Those daimyo who succumbed more enthusiastically than others to the pleasures of life in the capital and/or who indulged beyond their means in the conspicuous display that shogunal officials encouraged accumulated substantial debts to merchants. Many then launched austerity programs in their domains to increase the share of the annual tax revenue that was available to them, a measure which often imposed a disproportionate burden on their retainers and, over time, elicited criticism from within samurai ranks. That the heir to the headship of each daimyo house had grown up in Edo and had come to his domain for the first time upon his succession to the headship, a virtual stranger to many of those in his service, also tended to weaken the bonds between lord and vassal.

The third measure—or more accurately, set of measures—to note related to the separation of warriors and peasants. During the century of conflict that preceded the Tokugawa victory at

Sekigahara, many warriors lived in the countryside. Some were part-time farmers, who carried their weapons to the fields each day in case they were summoned to battle. Others were enfeoffed vassals of the daimyo they served. Their fiefs provided them with an independent source of wealth and manpower, and it was not uncommon for a vassal, Macbeth-like, to plot against his lord. *Gekokujō*, those below toppling those above, was the term used to describe this treacherous—and frequently successful—behavior.

To prevent such treachery, and to mobilize armed forces for the siege warfare which had been induced by the introduction of firearms by the Portuguese, some daimyo began giving their vassals military ranks and stipends instead of, or in addition to, fiefs and sought to concentrate all warriors in their service in a few strategically important places. Toyotomi Hideyoshi, who enjoyed a brief tenure as hegemon among the daimyo in the late sixteenth century, carried this process further by disarming the peasantry, from whose ranks many able fighters (including himself) had come.

Tokugawa Ieyasu and his successors encouraged these trends as an additional means of ensuring peace and stability, and by 1700 most samurai had been removed from the land. Daimyo were permitted only one castle in their domains, and samurai were required to live immediately outside its walls. In lieu of income from their own lands, they received an annual stipend in rice from domain coffers, its amount determined by their rank. Their status was hereditary, as was that of peasants, merchants, and artisans. No more 'disruptive' social mobility was to occur.

The removal of warriors from the land had profound consequences for Japan, extending far beyond what the Tokugawa had originally intended. In each of the more than 260 domains into which Japan was divided, a town developed around the daimyo's castle, its population consisting, roughly half and half, of stipended warriors and their families—a nascent urban consumer class—and of merchants and artisans who provided them with the goods and services they no longer could provide for themselves. Just as the system of alternate attendance stimulated commerce to serve the capital, the existence of at least one urban center in even the most remote corner of the country stimulated commercialization of the local economy.

Nor were merchants and artisans, known as townsmen (*chōnin*) and comprising perhaps 10 to 12 per cent of the population of Tokugawa Japan, the only commoners to benefit from the emerging political order. Although deprived of weapons and the chance—for a few—to achieve power and glory as successful warriors, the peasants of Japan, who constituted some 80 per cent of the total population, were also spared the disruptions of warfare and provided with new opportunities: to run village affairs on their own, within the limits ordained by the daimyo's officials but without constant supervision by those officials, who now lived in the castle town and visited them on periodic tours of inspection only; to grow fruits and vegetables for sale in the castle town or in one of the many new transit towns that served the needs of daimyo and their retinues en route to and from Edo, in addition to rice and other grains for their subsistence and for tax payments; and during the winter months or at other slack periods in the farming year to engage—surreptitiously, as it contravened their mandated role as food producers—in handicraft production to supply goods for sale to warriors or other commoners. By the mid-nineteenth century almost every one of the roughly 70,000 rural villages in Japan (though not every villager) was producing some sort of handicraft item for commercial sale, as well as producing ample crops to feed the nation and support its ruling élite.

As we shall see, the wealth accumulated by some peasants and townsmen as a result of this commercial activity was of growing concern to members of the warrior class and came to play a role in the events leading to the overthrow of the Tokugawa. Before turning to that subject, however, there is one more measure implemented early in the Tokugawa period to consider: the promotion of Neo-Confucianism as the official ideology of state.

No great religious causes or political ideas had fueled the conflict among competing daimyo in the century preceding the Tokugawa victory. Sheer survival, if not ever-greater power and influence, had been of primary concern. With peace, however, both the shogun and many of the daimyo came to perceive a need for some sort of justification for the new *status quo*. In particular, they worried about their retainers. Brave warriors, eager for battle and unafraid of death, had been of great value to them in the past, but would now prove a distinct liability. Something was required that would make the performance of peacetime duties as honorable as martial prowess and, by making loyalty to one's superior a living ideal, forever eliminate the threat of treachery from below.

They found the answer in Neo-Confucianism, a twelfth-century reformulation of classical Chinese Confucianism that had come to the attention of a few Buddhist monks in Japan during the century of warfare. A practical, this-worldly philosophy, Neo-Confucianism stressed the ethical nature of government: if rulers were virtuous—that is, if they were upright, loyal, and humane, as well as well-mannered and moderate in all things—good government would result and peace would prevail. Neo-Confucianism also stressed obedience to one's superiors: each person should perform the functions of his or her status in a natural social hierarchy, with subjects obeying rulers, sons obeying fathers, wives obeying husbands, and younger brothers obeying older.

Virtue did not occur naturally. It was acquired, by means of self-cultivation, formal education in the Confucian classics, and the study of the past in order to discover the basic principles governing human affairs. Japan's rulers ignored the meritocratic element within Neo-Confucianism, manifested in the examinations on the classics that were in theory open to any Chinese and that determined access to all posts in government, and continued to rely on heredity. Official posts in the shogunate and in the domains were open to members of the warrior class alone. But they embraced the cultivation of virtue with enthusiasm. Formal education was required of all samurai to enable them to perform the duties that were theirs by birth, and academies were established in Edo and in all the castle towns to provide it. Thus was set in motion another development with profound longer term consequences. By the early eighteenth century, rough, aggressive warriors throughout the entire country—not just in the capital—had been transformed into a literate political élite. Although the martial arts continued to be valued—indeed, extolled as defining elements of the way of the warrior, *bushidō*—members of the warrior class performed essentially civilian duties and, thanks to their education and socialization, derived an important measure of satisfaction and status honor from doing so. With the passage of each peaceful year, testimony in itself to the virtue of Japan's rulers and the legitimacy of their rule, warriors became bureaucrats.

The Meiji Restoration

It was the regime sketched above, which we can conceptualize as a prolonged stand-off between the competing pressures of decentralized feudalism and centralized monarchy,[4] that was cast aside in 1868 when the restoration of imperial rule was proclaimed. Despite the term 'restoration' and the use at first of some ancient precedents, the Meiji government took steps in its first decade of existence to transform the economy, society, and polity of Japan in ways that clearly resembled the thrust of bourgeois liberal revolutions in the eighteenth- and nineteenth-century West. In Japan, however, the bourgeoisie had little direct role in planning the transformation that ensued. The initiative for the overthrow of the Tokugawa and the leadership of the new imperial government came from within the warrior class—that is, from within the ruling élite. Moreover, among the reforms implemented by the new leadership were several that led fairly swiftly to the abolition of the special status that warriors (their own class) had enjoyed for centuries: in particular, their monopoly on government posts and the bearing of arms and their hereditary right to stipends. Such radicalism on the part of an incumbent ruling élite is unusual in the annals of human history. How is one to explain it?

That Japan's warrior class was divorced from the land was an important underlying factor. In contrast to traditional aristocracies elsewhere, warriors had no private estates in the countryside and, consequently, they lacked the personal, often passionate, commitment to the land and to a rural lifestyle that made many other aristocracies intensely conservative. Being relatively free of personal bias against economic change does not, however, explain why warriors—or more accurately, some warriors—advocated the economic transformation of the country, not to mention far-reaching political and social changes. To account for that we must examine, first, the discontent which developed among warriors in the latter half of the Tokugawa period and, second, the fairly swift emergence of reform-minded warriors to positions of influence in the newly formed Meiji government.

As mentioned earlier, the wealth accumulated by commoners was of growing concern to the ruling élite. In part, this was simply because that wealth violated the natural social hierarchy in which they believed. More tangibly, it was because of the economic problems it posed for them. Like many pensioners today, most samurai lived on fixed incomes; unlike pensioners, they expected to live a cut or more above the rest of the population. As commoners became more affluent and able to afford more of the goods and services once available to samurai alone, it became increasingly difficult for samurai to sustain an appropriately superior lifestyle. When some daimyo cut the stipends they paid their retainers, in order to generate resources for the repayment of their own growing debts, their retainers' standards of living, and self-esteem, were further reduced. A minor irritation for those few retainers with substantial stipends, this caused increasingly serious problems for the many with modest stipends.

With the diffusion of Neo-Confucian values among members of the warrior class, stipend reduction came to be attacked as morally wrong, on the grounds that the practice robbed innocent retainers of what was theirs by right in order to help profligate daimyo out of trouble. Nor was this the only way in which the education of warriors in Neo-Confucianism served to weaken, if not immediately to undermine, their respect for their superiors. Despite a proliferation of official posts in the first decades of the Tokugawa period, there were always fewer posts than samurai. Only one son, usually the first-born, inherited his father's samurai status, and his father's rank in most cases determined the range of offices for which he was eligible. Even then, he was only one of a pool of candidates for postings within that range. Taught that it was their duty to serve (the very meaning of the word samurai), many young warriors grew restive as they waited for official appointments. Others of modest rank who had out-performed the sons of higher ranking fathers in the domain academy were dismayed to discover that the important offices in the domain's administration were beyond their reach—and, indeed, were destined for those demonstrably less talented than they were. Thus began a questioning of the equation of rank with ability that culminated, for some, in the belief that the *higher* a warrior's rank, the *less* his ability. To describe a person as possessing 'a daimyo's skill' (*daimyō gei*) was not to convey a compliment.[5]

When efforts to reform the appointment system to give greater weight to ability regardless of rank came, essentially, to naught, not a few samurai concluded that their superiors lacked virtue. In Neo-Confucian terms, those superiors were defying Heaven's will. This was a conclusion rich in subversive implications, for it was imperative that unfit rulers be destroyed and Heaven's will served. As Sir George Sansom has observed, 'There can be no doubt that, of all the causes of the anti-Tokugawa, loyalist movement which ended in the fall of the [shogunate], the ambition of young samurai was the most powerful.'[6]

It was at this point, early in the nineteenth century, that Japan's ruling élite began to perceive a threat from outside the country's borders. Stemming first from isolated contacts with Russian adventurers and then from news of the Opium Wars in China, the threat culminated in 1853 with the arrival of Commodore Perry's squadron and the American demand that the shogunate open the country to commercial contact. The shogunate's reluctant agreement to this demand, and to the similar demands it soon received from other Western countries, provided a focus for much of the discontent that had been brewing for decades. However rational its decision may have been, the shogunate had opened itself to charges of dereliction of duty. Rather than quelling the Western 'barbarians', one of the historic tasks of an emperor's chief military deputy, the shogun had bowed to their demands. His military weakness—and hence his vulnerability to domestic rivals, as well as to the barbarians—had been revealed.

Not all samurai took an active part in the ensuing years of intrigue and activism which resulted in the collapse of the shogunate and the restoration of imperial rule. By far the greatest number came from only four domains in south-western Japan: Satsuma, Chōshū, Tosa, and Hizen. Nor, in its early phases, was the anti-Tokugawa, pro-emperor movement confined to samurai. Some daimyo played leading roles, as did a small group of nobles from the emperor's court in Kyoto.

The shifting alliances, miscalculations, and confrontations of this eventful period must not detain us here. The important point to note is that, as in many political upheavals, a diversity of motives and objectives came into play. Some participants wished to expell the barbarians at all costs, others to obtain revenge for the defeat of their ancestors by Tokugawa Ieyasu at Sekigahara all those many years ago; still others thought only of elevating the emperor to his rightful place as ruler of all Japan. What was muted, to say the least, in the agitation and sloganeering of the day was the call for sweeping reforms of the sort that later took place. Attention focused on toppling the Tokugawa shogunate, not on Japan's post-Tokugawa future.

It was only when Tokugawa Yoshinobu resigned in 1867 that those who had led the struggle against him were forced to confront that future. Would a new shogunate be formed, headed by the daimyo of one of the leading anti-Tokugawa domains? Or a federation of domains, including perhaps the Tokugawa house, with the daimyo forming some sort of council at the apex of a new, nominally imperial government? When and how would the Western barbarians be expelled? That domains themselves would be eliminated, along with the status of daimyo, was inconceivable to many, as was the further opening of the country to the West and the definition of Japan as the 'barbarian' country in need of civilization and enlightenment.

A fragile coalition at first, containing men with very different ideas of Japan's future course, the new Meiji government was threatened with paralysis, and quite possibly with disintegration. That it survived this threat and embarked on a program of sweeping reforms can be attributed to the political acumen and pragmatism of a relatively small number of samurai. From subordinate positions in the new regime in January 1868, they had risen by late 1869 to its leadership. Only then did the revolution begin.

In 1868 the top posts in the new government were, without exception, held by daimyo, court nobles, and imperial princes. Samurai were to be found only as junior councilors and aides. By the summer of 1869, however, only a very few daimyo remained in office. Other than a small number of court nobles, all key posts in the emerging administrative structure were now held by samurai. Principally from the domains of Satsuma, Chōshū, Tosa, and Hizen, most of the latter were in their thirties or early forties and of middling rank. The majority had held posts in their respective domains before the Restoration, acquiring practical experience in administration. Not unimportantly, they had honed their political skills in the turbulent last years of the shogunate. By using those skills effectively, they were able to outmaneuver the men to whom the top posts had initially been given, luring them into retirement with honors and guaranteed incomes, and secure real power themselves.

Many of these samurai had become convinced that the problems facing Japan—of dealing with the Westerners now in their midst and coping with the economic dislocations caused by unregulated foreign trade, for example—could not be solved by action at the domain level. As the problems were national in scope, national solutions were required. Some had traveled to the West in the early 1860s and seen at first hand the factories, railways, and political institutions that made Western nations so powerful. Japan's best defense against the West, they concluded, lay in developing comparable power. With little attachment to the old order—indeed, with accumulated grievances against it—and with a deeply ingrained bureaucratic orientation toward problem-solving, they turned their attention to creating a new Japan.

2 | Creating the New Nation

Although critical of Japan's past under the Tokugawa shogunate, the leaders of the new Meiji government were themselves products of that past. Despite their willingness to innovate in many respects, they could not instantly shed their own upbringing and socialization. To an important extent, then, they were guided by the norms and values of the warrior class in creating a new Japan.

Those norms and values were not, it should be remembered, exclusively or even primarily martial. The long years of peace and the system of warrior education during the Tokugawa period had imbued warriors with a civil-service ethic. What remained of an earlier, warlike ethos served mainly to buttress their role as hereditary bureaucrats: an emphasis on discipline, a disdain for creature comforts, inheritance of the property and headship of the family by a single son, and marriage as an instrument to produce that son.

The samurai who rose to leadership of the new Meiji government not only subscribed to these norms and values; they also sought to extend them to the population as a whole. One major consequence, then, of the leading role played by members of the warrior class in the Restoration and in the new Meiji state was the partial 'samuraization' of Japan.

The patriarchal family of the warrior became the model for all families, displacing in law if not always in reality the looser, more flexible practices of marriage and inheritance that had long prevailed among commoners, especially in the countryside. Frivolity and fun were denigrated, and austerity and discipline extolled.

Loyalty and service, now to the emperor rather than to daimyo or shogun, were demanded from everyone. Although hereditary status distinctions were abolished, commoners had to prove their merit before the élite would surrender any of the awesome responsibilities of national government to them. Until that time—and the men at the helm of early Meiji Japan were convinced that considerable time would be required—power would remain where it had always been, in the hands of officials.

There was nothing casual about the leadership's attempts to extend their ethos to the population as a whole. From the outset they felt a sense of urgency about the task. Nor was it an easy matter. One of the more persistent myths about late nineteenth-century Japan is that ordinary Japanese—the townsmen and peasants of the Tokugawa era, now the free and equal subjects of the emperor—were uniquely docile and submissive. The leaders of the new regime were thus spared one of the key problems of nation-building elsewhere in the world: they did not have to worry about popular attitudes and aspirations. Lemming-like, the people would follow wherever led, and financial resources which might have been needed for keeping the peace domestically could be used to promote economic development and the attainment of other national goals.

It is true that Japan's development in the late nineteenth and early twentieth centuries did not give rise to the massive social and political disruption that occurred in some other modernizing societies. Rather than being a given of Japan's development, however, this was an outcome of policy and effort. Government officials had been concerned about the ordinary people of Japan from the early 1870s onward, and they took a variety of deliberate steps to create and sustain popular identification with the state. It was their successful management of the disappointments and grievances engendered by modernization that kept social and political disruption within bounds. Conflict was not eliminated completely, as we shall see in Chapter 4, but it could be fairly swiftly isolated and contained. Before considering the specific measures implemented by government officials, let us examine the sources of their concern.

If by the word 'nation' we mean a politically organized community of people who share a common language and culture, then Japan in 1868 clearly does not measure up. Quite apart from the problems of political organization facing the new regime at the center of the polity, the people were divided by differences in dialect and strong ties to the villages and neighborhoods in which their families had lived for centuries. Although many ordinary Japanese welcomed the lifting of long-standing barriers to occupational mobility, they remained attached to the pastimes and traditions of the status group in which they had been raised. Their distrust of warriors, as tax collectors who would take from them the fruits of their labor, carried over into a suspicion of the new government and the burdens it would impose.

These attitudes soon became apparent to officials in the Meiji government as they attempted to collect taxes on former Tokugawa lands, the first to come under their control, and later as they attempted to redraw the administrative map of Japan, replacing the domains of the past with a much smaller number of prefectures. Although the daimyo accepted posts as the appointed governors of their former domains without demur and then accepted retirement on comfortable pensions when the domains were consolidated into prefectures, commoners in some parts of the country protested the new boundaries, especially when they found themselves liable for taxes at the higher rate that had prevailed in one or more neighboring jurisdictions.

Unsurprisingly perhaps, ordinary Japanese did not automatically welcome news of the Conscription Ordinance of 1873, which made all young men over the age of 20 liable to service in a new national army. True, commoners thus regained a long-lost equality with samurai, but what caught their attention was the reference, in instructions from Tokyo for implementing the new policy at the local level, to conscription as a 'blood tax' that every man should pay to the state. Taking this literally, they saw conscription as an immediate threat to the lives of their sons and needed persuading that this was not the case before they would comply. Even then, many resented the loss, however temporary, of able-bodied labor on the farm or in the family business. Similarly, although not necessarily opposed to education for their children, many ordinary Japanese noted with alarm that localities, not the state, would have to bear the cost of constructing schools and that parents would have to pay tuition fees.

To officials used to governing the people by fiat, not persuasion, and intent on realizing their avowed goal of 'making the country prosper and strengthening its defenses' (*fukoku kyōhei*), popular indifference to their initiatives was almost as disturbing as popular resistance. The people were dangerously parochial, officials concluded, concerned only with their own lives or their own local communities and insensitive to the needs of 'Japan'. That they persisted in such 'evil practices of the past' as lewd dancing at harvest festivals or stripping down to loincloths when hauling goods through city streets in summer was further evidence of their ignorance of the challenges facing the country. How could the Meiji leadership secure equal and respectful treatment of Japan by Western governments when such examples of the country's continued backwardness were there for Western diplomats to see?

A renewed sense of urgency was added to these initial concerns roughly a generation later, as officials came to perceive that Western countries faced problems at home that should serve as a warning to Japan and, not unimportantly, as the demands of empire made unity and discipline seem even more essential than before. On the whole, the first Japanese who had travelled abroad after the ending of national seclusion had been awed into uncritical admiration by the visible strength and vitality of the Western countries they toured. Only later, and with no little assistance from Western informants, did Japanese visitors come to see the problems that coexisted with, indeed were caused by, progress in those same countries: the breakup of rural communities, new forms of poverty and deprivation in cities, class strife, labor unrest, even the threat of revolution. Not a few able young men sent by the government to study at German universities in the late nineteenth century were persuaded by the social policy ideas then in vogue. Developed by Gustav von Schmoller and other academic members of the Verein für Sozialpolitik, these called for intervention by the state in economic and social affairs so that the problems caused by industrialization could be overcome. An enlightened bureaucracy which stood above class interests and acted on behalf of the entire nation was the best instrument for reconciling opposing social forces and achieving social justice. When these young men returned home and took up posts in the Japanese bureaucracy, they had a chance to implement these ideas, and ample motivation to do so.

Sharing with Marx the view that 'the industrially more developed country presents to the less developed country a picture of the latter's future', they nevertheless rejected the notion that this was an iron law of history. On the contrary, as one Japanese bureaucrat observed in 1896, 'it is the advantage of the backward country that it can *reflect* on the history of the advanced countries *and avoid their mistakes*'.[1] Japan could learn from the 'sad and pitiful'[2] history of industrialization in Britain, for example, and take steps in good time to secure a different, less volatile outcome from economic growth.

The perceived demands of Japan's newly acquired colonial empire and its other regional interests added to the bureaucracy's intensified concern with the people. Although Japan had won the Sino-Japanese War of 1894–5 fairly easily, its resources were strained to the limit by the Russo-Japanese War a decade later. Only the ability to muster all the material and spiritual strength of the nation, it was asserted, had permitted victory. Convinced that a czarist war of revenge was inevitable, officials argued that there could be no respite. In addition to increased spending on the army and navy, it was essential that the people be kept united and their patriotic willingness to pay higher taxes sustained.

Now let us consider the specific steps the government took from early in the Meiji era through about 1910 to combat parochialism and secure popular identification with the state. First, officials sought to promote popular awareness of and identification with the monarchy. 'Revere the emperor' (*sonnō*) had been one of two potent rallying cries of the anti-Tokugawa movement in the 1860s. Linked with the other, 'Expel the barbarians' (*jōi*), it had given discontented warriors a justification for what amounted to acts of disloyalty against their more immediate superiors. The commoner population had not been a target of this rallying cry, however, and when the Restoration was proclaimed few ordinary Japanese had any inkling of who or what had been restored. After all, the emperors had lived in obscurity in Kyoto for centuries, and the world of most commoners extended only so far as a nearby village or market town.

That Mutsuhito, the Meiji emperor, was only a callow youth of 16 in 1868 may have made it easier for the emerging leaders of the Restoration government to define his place in the new state pretty much as they saw fit, but it also meant that one of the few strengths they possessed at the outset, the source of their own legitimacy, did not cut a very imposing figure. They soon set about remedying this situation. What began as efforts to induce the daimyo to support the new regime and, not unimportantly, to impress Westerners gradually extended to efforts to capture the hearts and minds of the people.

In place of the annual allowance on which it had depended during the Tokugawa period, the imperial household was given its own sources of wealth—initially, tracts of farmland and forests; later, stocks and bonds—so that it could afford an appropriately dignified lifestyle and elaborate ceremonies. The emperor himself was given new clothes, specially designed Western-style military uniforms as well as fashionable suits, to serve as a visible symbol of the new directions his country was taking. He was sent on tours and progresses throughout the country, to make himself known to his people. Some of the religious ceremonies Japan's emperors had always performed were now made public, and both the Meiji emperor's birthday and imperial foundation day (11 February, *kigensetsu*, said to be the date when the first emperor had descended from heaven in 660 BC) were given pride of place in a new calendar of national holidays. Impressive proclamations and edicts were issued in the emperor's name, calling upon the people to support the building of schools, hospitals, and factories and to render service to Japan.

As time passed, the latter theme of service to Japan received increasing emphasis in imperial pronouncements. A prime example was the Imperial Rescript on Education, issued in 1890, which read:

Know ye, Our subjects:
Our Imperial Ancestors have founded Our Empire on a basis broad and everlasting, and have deeply and firmly implanted virtue: Our subjects ever united in loyalty and filial piety have from generation to generation illustrated the beauty thereof. This is the glory of the fundamental character of Our Empire, and herein also lies the source of Our education. Ye, Our subjects, be filial to your parents, affectionate to your brothers and sisters; as husbands and wives be harmonious, as friends true; bear yourselves in modesty and moderation; extend your benevolence to all; pursue learning and cultivate arts, and therefore develop intellectual faculties and perfect moral powers; furthermore, advance public good and promote common interests; always respect the Constitution and observe the laws; should emergency arise, offer yourselves courageously to the State; and thus guard and maintain the prosperity of Our Imperial Throne coeval with heaven and earth. So shall ye be not only Our good and faithful subjects, but render illustrious the best traditions of your forefathers . . .[3]

Although concerned with educational policy and directed, initially, at pupils and teachers in the nation's schools (about which more below), this rescript also functioned as a statement of ethical principles, of a sort which any samurai of the late Tokugawa period would have recognized, for the population as a whole. In its reference to the 'best traditions' of the past and in its general thrust, it reflected the desire on the part of Japan's leaders, after more than two decades of new departures, to slow the pace of change and, by enshrining their values as the values of the nation, to protect Japan from the disruptive consequences of progress.

The Boshin Rescript of 1908, which reflected the government's determination to mobilize the people for the tasks facing their country in the aftermath of the Russo-Japanese War, provided a more somber enumeration of their obligations:

We desire all classes of Our people to act in unison, to be faithful to their callings, frugal in the management of their households, submissive to the dictates of conscience and calls of duty, frank and sincere in their manners, to abide by simplicity and avoid ostentation, and to inure themselves to arduous toil without yielding to any degree of indulgence. . . . By scrupulous observances of the precepts thus established, the growing prosperity of Our Empire is assured.[4]

The second step officials took was to modify the content of instruction in the country's elementary schools so that appropriate values as well as basic literacy and numeracy would be acquired by all children. Construction of elementary schools had proceeded apace in the 1870s, despite initial objections from some members of the public about the financial burdens imposed on them. The enrollment of all boys and girls was made compulsory in 1879, and the mandatory period of schooling was gradually extended from sixteen months (over four years) in 1879 to four years in 1886 and six years in 1907. Actual rates of attendance rose rather slowly, from 35 per cent of those of statutory age in 1875 to 49 per cent in 1890. Not until 1910, a few years after the elimination of all tuition fees, were well-nigh universal rates of attendance achieved.

At first there had been a substantial Western thrust to much of the knowledge youngsters acquired. Indeed, in the haste to get the school system up and running, some Western textbooks had been quickly translated into Japanese by the Ministry of Education and distributed throughout the country. These included the *Marius Wilson Readers* from the United States, amply illustrated with scenes from everyday American life, and portions of a French text intended to teach French youngsters to respect God and the laws of the Second Republic.

By the mid-1870s officials in Tokyo had begun to realize that an opportunity to promote a sense of national identity among the younger generation was being missed. Thereafter, heroes and role models from Japan's own past, not only from the West's, began to appear more frequently in the textbooks the Ministry of Education itself produced. In the early 1880s, officials in the ministry began to exert control over textbook selection, which had previously been left to prefectural authorities. From evaluating existing texts, many of them published by firms in the private sector, and recommending titles to prefectural officials, they moved first to issuing guidelines for the content of textbooks and then, after the revelation in 1903 of widespread bribery of prefectual officials by textbook publishers eager to have their books chosen, to the selection and subsequently the writing of most textbooks within the ministry itself.

Teacher training, placement, and promotion were also put under central government control, and government inspectors were appointed to monitor the implementation of the state's educational policies at the local level. While Western material did not disappear completely from textbooks, and while training in practical skills still remained an important part of the curriculum, from the 1880s greater emphasis was placed on inculcating loyalty to the emperor and filial piety, especially in the ethics classes which all pupils attended for two hours a week. This trend was accelerated by the issuance of the Imperial Rescript on Education in 1890. A copy of the rescript and a portrait of the emperor were sent to every school in the country, where they were reverentially employed in annual ceremonies of patriotism. In the new regulations for elementary schools announced in 1891, the Ministry of Education declared: 'In education, the greatest attention should be paid to moral culture. Hence, whatever is found, in *any* course of study, relating to moral or national education should be taught with care and assiduity.'[5] Thereafter, texts for the study of the Japanese language, which occupied pupils for about ten hours per week, began to feature material extolling loyalty, filial piety, and other approved virtues to a greater extent than previously.

Third, officials took steps to incorporate the local communities of Japan into the emerging administrative structures of the central government and to make those communities, and their residents, as responsive as possible to central direction.

After an unsuccessful attempt in the early 1870s to bypass existing rural towns and villages and impose a completely new system of large and small districts (*ku*) within the prefectures, government officials set about making towns and villages into what they considered to be acceptable units of administration. In each unit a revenue base had to be created that was large enough to support such new tasks as the construction and maintenance of school buildings, the promotion of public health, and the preliminary screening of young men for military service. To that end, a massive program of amalgamation was carried out, by which the borders of towns were extended to include nearby villages and neighboring villages were combined into one. As a result, the total number of officially recognized towns and villages was reduced from about 80,000 in 1874 to a little over 15,000 in 1889 and to roughly 12,000 in 1905. These newly amalgamated towns and villages had to perform the tasks desired by officials in Tokyo, rather than embarking on projects of their own. This was achieved by means of the Town and Village Code of 1888, and subsequent legislation, which assigned a large number of obligatory tasks to the localities, defined the kind and extent of taxes they could levy, and provided for supervision of their activities by prefectural officials and, ultimately, by the Home Ministry in Tokyo.

It is worth noting that the Meiji government did not find it easy to create these acceptable units of administration. Lacking both money and staff in the early 1870s, it had been forced initially to seek the co-operation of the wealthy merchants and farmers who had long run town and village affairs, and those men in turn had exploited the leverage they gained to delay boundary changes that affected them adversely and to press for a formal role in local and prefectural politics. Only after some two decades of effort (longer by far than it had taken to dispossess the daimyo) and some carefully calibrated concessions—e.g. the creation of elected village, town, and prefectural assemblies, each with very limited powers and with members chosen only or primarily by the propertied few—did the government have its way.

And despite Tokyo's hard-won success, the old, 'natural' villages of the Tokugawa period did not disappear. Although lacking any formal role in the new local government system, they continued to exist as distinct settlements, or hamlets, within 'administrative' towns or villages. Many of them still owned such communal property as forests, wells, cemeteries, and shrines—the result of the government's desire to minimize resistance to amalgamation in the 1880s and 1890s—and most still functioned as the center of the economic and social life of their inhabitants. It was to this situation that the government turned its attention in the years following the Russo-Japanese War of 1904–5.

Some 80 per cent of the Japanese people still lived in the countryside at that time. If their loyalties could be directed outward from the hamlet to the town or village of which they were nominally a part, then the state could influence them through its control of local government. More directly, if the state could exert bureaucratic guidance over some of the 'rice roots' organizations that existed in rural communities, it could mobilize those organizations and their members into service to the nation. A powerful bulwark against the radical ideologies that might well find their way to Japanese cities could therefore be erected.

As part of the local improvement movement the government sponsored in the early 1900s, a renewed attempt was made to transfer all hamlet property to towns and villages, and in 1906 a campaign of shrine mergers was launched. The many hamlet shrines in existence, which were devoted to such intensely local concerns as healthy children and good crops, were to be destroyed and a single shrine established in each village. The central village shrine would then serve as a symbol both of the corporate life of the village as a whole and, by means of linkages with prefectural and national shrines in the emerging system of State Shinto, of the village's larger obligations to Japan.

Owing in large measure to protests from small farmers, who depended on access to the communal lands in their hamlets for economic survival, and to the refusal of many hamlets to abandon shrines as commanded, the government made only limited progress in these aspects of its renewed assault on the parochialism of rural Japanese. It enjoyed considerable success, however, in its efforts to influence the community-based organizations to which they belonged.

The local farming societies that had been formed in some communities during the 1880s and 1890s were co-opted into the Imperial Agricultural Association, a nationwide federation, and in 1905 all farm households were required to join its local branches. Local credit and mutual aid associations, which traced their origins to the Tokugawa period, were now championed as model agencies for promoting diligence and frugality among the people and were co-opted into a national organization in 1906. The young men's groups that existed in most hamlets, where they performed such useful tasks as fire fighting and carrying the community's portable shrine in local festivals, were reorganized into village associations and given new activities of a patriotic sort: regular calisthenics to encourage discipline and prepare their members for their pre-conscription physical examinations; lectures on ethics; a role in ceremonies in honor of the emperor at the village school. Local veterans' clubs, some of them dating from the late 1870s and many others established after the Russo-Japanese War to help soldiers readjust to civilian life, were reorganized into local branches of a nationwide Imperial Military Reservists' Association in 1910. In addition to continued military training to prepare them for an eventual recall to active duty, reservists were expected to supervise the local young men's association, provide disaster relief, and play a prominent part in patriotic ceremonies in their communities.

The Meiji emperor died on 30 July 1912, after forty-five years on the throne. Even allowing for a degree of hyperbole in contemporary reports, it appears that ordinary Japanese throughout the country were stunned by news of his final illness and death. Long before official instructions were dispatched, telling them how to behave, they began to mourn their loss. That in itself is testimony to the success of official efforts to promote popular identification with the monarchy. Virtually unknown to his people at the time of the Restoration, the emperor had become an eminent and potent figure, of whom everyone was aware.

Japanese officials had not invented this particular nation-building strategy, nor indeed had they invented any of the other strategies they employed in the late nineteenth and early twentieth centuries. Monarchy was a proven instrument for creating and sustaining national unity in roughly a dozen Western countries. Similarly, the inculcation of patriotism and other approved values was widely regarded in the West as one of the proper functions of primary education. Creating an effective relationship between central and local government institutions, and between central government and the people, had occupied the attention of the leaders of every new nation state. Although Bismarck's Germany had led the way in implementing social policies to deal with poverty, labor unrest, and other divisive consequences of industrialization, advocates of similar measures to deal with such problems were to be found in Britain and the United States as well as in Japan.

What was unusual about Japan was the timing and the rigorous application of these strategies. Determined to profit from the experience of the advanced nations of the West, Japan's leaders acted not to cure the perceived evils of development, but to prevent those evils from arising. By seizing the initiative and acting before powerful lobbies and interest groups were formed, they enjoyed a comparatively free hand in implementing policies as they saw fit.

By means of the linkages that were established with schools and with a variety of local organizations, officials were able to monitor popular thought and behavior. If unacceptable attitudes or conduct surfaced among the people, they were likely to learn of them swiftly. This was a change from the Tokugawa period, when official linkages with the commoner population were either weak or non-existent and when popular grievances often festered unnoticed. Those who ruled Japan then could be surprised by peasant uprisings or other popular disturbances, but no longer. With early warning of what they considered to be dangerous trends and with channels of communication and influence already in place, officials in the Meiji period and beyond could impose countermeasures when and as they wished, long before armed suppression was the only option available to them.

3

Toward an Industrial Economy

*I*n addition to providing a focus for the discontent that had been brewing for decades among members of the warrior élite, the shogunate's agreement in the mid-1850s to Western demands for the abandonment of national seclusion led to unsettling pressures on Japan's economy. The carefully regulated trade with the outside world that had operated since the early seventeenth century was brought to an abrupt end by the signing of commercial treaties with a succession of Western states and the arrival of Western traders to take up residence and pursue business in the ports those treaties had opened to them. Japan's coinage and its reserves of precious metals were suddenly exposed to an internationally accepted ratio between gold and silver that differed markedly and unfavorably from the ratio established by fiat within the country. Domestic handicraft products, and their numerous producers, were almost as suddenly exposed to competition from cheaper and generally higher quality goods manufactured in Europe and the United States, and because the tariffs that Japan could charge on imports were set at a low level by the commercial treaties the shogunate had signed, there was little scope for protecting domestic producers from that competition.

Viewed from the perspective of the experience of such other non-Western countries as China, Peru, or Egypt during the nineteenth century, the situation in which Japan found itself as it was brusquely incorporated into an international economy dominated by the industrialized nations of the West was fraught with peril.

The most likely outcome was a descent into semi-colonial status, with its economy increasingly geared to the needs of one or more foreign powers and its sovereignty over domestic institutions increasingly impaired. The least likely outcome—in that no non-Western country had yet managed it, and not a few Western countries were finding the effort difficult—was an ascent into the ranks of the industrial élite.

That Japan managed, eventually, to achieve the latter outcome has attracted considerable scholarly attention, and deservedly so. This was the true economic 'miracle' of modern Japanese history, which not only defied the apparent logic of Japan's situation at the time but also created much of the basis for Japan's rise to 'economic superpower' status in the decades following its defeat in the Second World War. In this chapter I will examine, in a fairly unsystematic way and without resort to statistical tables, econometric models, or, except in the most general terms, theories of economic development, a number of reasons why Japan was able to achieve this unprecedented outcome.

Before that, a few comments about the pace of Japan's economic transformation are in order. What we are dealing with is a fairly long and unsteady process, not a dramatically rapid 'take-off' of the sort that would have pleased the World Bank in the 1960s, much less a dramatically rapid shift to a new economic structure. Japan's economy continued basically unchanged for two decades or more after the Meiji Restoration. Even in the late 1930s, some sixty years after the leaders of the Meiji government had decided to promote industrialization, Japan was still a junior member of the industrial élite, ranking sixteenth—just slightly ahead of the Soviet Union but behind Italy—in gross national product per capita. Although large-scale, capital-intensive enterprises were now growing at a rapid pace, more people still gained their livelihoods from agriculture than from industry, and within the industrial sector a declining but important share of total output was supplied by small, poorly equipped workshops employing fewer than five persons. The 'miracle', then, was not in the suddenness of movement from a traditionally agrarian to a modern industrial economy, but in the movement *per se*. A notoriously difficult undertaking—stymied elsewhere in what we would now term the developing world by a wide range of economic, political, and social factors—was well under way, and indeed had been gaining momentum since the 1890s.

The International Environment

'God grant that in opening their country to the West we may not be bringing upon them misery and ruin.' So wrote Lord Elgin, negotiator of Britain's Treaty of Peace, Amity, and Commerce with Japan, in his private journal in 1858.[1] His concern was atypical (and not replicated in his public utterances) at a time when his fellow countrymen regarded commerce and free trade as great achievements of Western civilization and the path to peace and prosperity throughout the world, but no doubt it reflected his observations elsewhere in Asia—in China, in particular—where events seemed to contradict Western optimism as far as the indigenous populations were concerned.

Elgin's treaty was the second of sixteen that Japan signed with Western states, and like the others it contained a number of provisions that soon came to be perceived by the Japanese as 'unequal': extraterritoriality (or consular jurisdiction), conventional tariffs, and the granting of most favored nation status. Extraterritoriality meant that British residents of the ports which Japan had opened to trade and foreign residence were subject to the jurisdiction of the British authorities and to trial by the British consul, according to the laws of Great Britain, if they committed any crime against Japanese subjects or the subjects or citizens of any other country. The treaty also restricted the tariffs that Japan could impose on imports from Britain and exports to Britain to those agreed by the authorities of the two countries and enumerated in a detailed convention. Most favored nation status required that any privilege, immunity, or advantage granted by Japan to the government or nationals of any other country—for example, the opening of additional ports and foreign settlements or, as many Westerners sought, the lifting of the restrictions on their movement beyond the confines of the treaty ports on which

38 Toward an Industrial Economy

the Japanese negotiators had insisted—be automatically extended to the British government and its subjects. None of these provisions was reciprocal; that is, Japanese nationals in Britain were not governed by the laws of Japan, British tariffs on Japanese goods were not subject to Japanese approval, and Japan was not granted most favored nation status by Britain.

These provisions were key elements in the diplomacy of imperialism which Western nations had honed in their dealings with Japan's 'backward' and 'barbaric' neighbors in Asia earlier in the nineteenth century, and they set in motion the same dynamics in Japan that had led to further impairments of sovereignty and loss of control over the domestic economy elsewhere. Very swiftly, Westerners came to dominate Japan's trade with the outside world. Not only did Western ships transport virtually all goods entering or leaving Japan, or going by sea from one part of Japan to another; in addition, Western trading houses in the treaty ports made the vast majority of all transactions with Japanese wholesalers, charging pre-payment on import orders, and paying considerably less than prevailing world prices for export goods. As noted above, Westerners were not content to remain in the treaty ports and pressed actively for free access to the interior of Japan, to seek converts to their religion and direct deals with the producers of export commodities. Within the ports themselves, they made efforts to establish tea-processing plants and other factories, so as to garner even greater profits for themselves. Not only Japan's foreign trade but also modern economic enterprise itself might have ended up in Western hands, within a string of treaty settlements along the coast, had these dynamics continued unimpeded.

There was, however, a brighter side to the situation. Broadly speaking, the international economy of the mid- to late nineteenth century was not unfavorable to a would-be aspirant to industrial status. Apart from the occasional war or local economic crisis, it was an era of overall economic expansion in the developed world and in international trade. Despite the impediments imposed by colonial preference and the desire to protect a few strategic industries, the ideology of free trade had powerful champions in Europe and North America, most notably in the

United Kingdom and the United States. With the railway age in full sway and Western confidence in industrialism soaring, there were relatively few barriers, economically or psychologically, to the entry of a new participant. Perhaps not until the late 1940s, in the aftermath of the Second World War and the beginnings of widespread movement toward decolonization and assistance in development, were prevailing circumstances as auspicious.

Given the relatively recent invention and relative simplicity of many industrial technologies in the nineteenth century, the gap to be closed by a new aspirant to industrial status may well have been narrower than at any time since. That the Japanese islands lay athwart what were then becoming the major trade routes of the Western Pacific and were well situated by this accident of geography for contact with both Asia and the United States were further advantages, as was a timely outbreak of silkworm disease in Europe just as Japan was groping for a way to earn foreign exchange to permit the purchase of modern military and industrial technology.

Japan's Potential for Industrial Development

Of course, it was by no means pre-ordained that Japan would find the advantages in its situation, while avoiding the most serious pitfalls. One underlying factor of considerable importance in enabling it to do so was the economic and social legacy of the Tokugawa past.

As noted in Chapter 1, national seclusion during the centuries of Tokugawa ascendancy did not lead to the economic stagnation many nineteenth-century Westerners assumed. On the contrary, output increased and the economy became steadily more commercialized during the long years of peace, in response to new incentives to produce agricultural and handicraft goods for sale. Yet the economy remained essentially unchanged in structure.

The vast majority of the population worked in agriculture, employing labor-intensive technology on small-scale farms, and their output formed a major proportion of total output. There was a non-agricultural sector, to be sure, consisting of crafts and services, but here too small units of production and labor-intensive methods prevailed. Although there were tools aplenty, little in the way of machinery was used in the manufacture of textiles, paper, ceramics, and other goods; steam power, which did so much to boost the productivity of labor during the industrial revolutions of the West, was unknown. Land transport was mainly by bearer or horse, with the mountainous terrain and the existence of official barriers at strategic points along the way further impeding the rapid and cost-efficient movement of commodities. Coastal shipping by sailing junk flourished for the transport of bulk cargoes, but the shogunate's restrictions on the size of vessels that could be constructed, as well as the difficulties of navigating Japanese coastal waters, necessitated frequent stops at night and in bad weather. As in farming, the level of output per capita in the non-agricultural sector was held back to a relatively low level, depending as it did on the skills of individual workers, unaided by much in the way of labor-boosting devices. In short, with every passing day, a better, larger, more efficient, and more commercialized preindustrial agrarian economy was emerging, but without new incentives, including the lifting of ideological and institutional constraints, and without new inputs of technology and capital, a preindustrial agrarian economy it was likely to remain.

What was significant about this late Tokugawa economy, so far as the subsequent industrial development of Japan is concerned, may be summarized as follows. First, there was still some scope for further growth in output in the agricultural sector. Like industrial economies today, agrarian economies of the past differed from one another in the extent of their development. Had there been a league table of agrarian economies at the time, Japan's might have ranked somewhere in the upper middle level, well above economies that experienced frequent subsistence crises but still not at the limits of expansion by pre-existing, preindustrial means. This meant that more food could be produced by the application of more hours of labor to the land and by the diffusion of the fairly simple improvements in seed selection, planting, and controlling weeds or insects that had been devised by some farmers in highly commercialized regions to farmers everywhere in the country. By exploiting this remaining growth potential, a process which did not cost very much at all in monetary terms, Japan remained able to feed its population during the Meiji era. Resources that other developing countries then and since have had to devote to massive capital spending on a faltering agricultural sector and/or to imports of food could be (and were) diverted to other ends.

Second, the slow but fairly steady expansion of the late Tokugawa economy created surpluses above subsistence needs that could be (and were) utilized as a domestic source of capital for industrial development. For reasons that still remain somewhat obscure, but that probably owed more to the positive choices made by millions of Japanese than to cruel necessity,[2] the population of Japan remained fairly stable at 30 to 33 million throughout the second half of the Tokugawa period, that is, from the early eighteenth to the mid-nineteenth centuries. The result was an increase in per capita income. Because the economic 'pie' was expanding in size, the 'slices' available, in theory, to each and every Japanese became larger. Had these slices been equally available in practice to one and all, they might have been consumed forthwith—dissipated in a myriad relatively slight improvements in living standards—but they were not. While many Japanese commoners held their own at best and, as noted earlier, many samurai struggled to make ends meet, some among the commoner population in both urban and rural Japan benefited more or less handsomely, accumulating wealth beyond their daily needs and—given the social policy of the warrior class—well beyond what they could safely display in conspicuous consumption. Their savings and/or the profits they earned from investment in land reclamation, money-lending, new branches of their businesses, or new forms of cottage industry formed a potential pool of capital for an industrializing Japan. At a time when overseas development aid from Western governments was unknown, and when the private financial markets of the West demanded a high price not only in interest but also in collateral from borrowers, this was to prove a valuable legacy indeed.

Third, a reservoir of attitudes and skills existed among the Japanese people by the end of the Tokugawa period which served in important ways to narrow the distance Japan had to travel in industrializing. Owing to prosperity as well as to the trickle-down effects of warrior benevolence, there was considerable literacy among the commoner population. An estimated 40 per cent of males and 15 per cent of females had received or were receiving some degree of formal schooling by the 1860s, fairly high levels for a preindustrial country and a useful foundation for the universal education system the state was to begin creating roughly a decade later. Affluent commoners put their literacy to use not only in reading popular fiction and Confucian tracts, but also in keeping business records or monitoring the results of their experiments with new crops. The idea that one could gain useful information from written records, so vital to the mastering of new scientific and technological knowledge, was steadily taking root.

In addition, farmers as well as city dwellers in many parts of the country had gained experience in producing commodities for commercial sale and were, within the limits imposed by domain officials and some entrenched urban guilds, increasingly responsive to market stimuli. As noted earlier, many farmers also engaged part-time in non-agricultural occupations. Although this could occur in their farmhouses, during the evenings or the winter months, for an increasing number of farmers it came to involve traveling a distance during the agricultural slack season and working for the wages, and usually the accommodation, meals, and other support services, provided by an employer. As we shall see, much of the industrial labor force of late nineteenth-century Japan came from farm families, and although the process of converting these rural recruits into industrial workers was not trouble-free, it was certainly easier than it might have been had the Japanese countryside remained untouched by economic change.

One of the major at-home by-employments of farm families in some parts of the country was sericulture: the raising of silk-worms and hand-reeling of raw silk. A task usually left to women, sericulture equipped Japan with a potential export product that could be, and was, expanded and improved in response to Western demand. The reeling and weaving skills of rural women, and the continuing need of farm families for additional cash income, were important factors in providing Japan with a vital source of export earnings after the ending of national seclusion. Indeed, raw silk provided roughly 30 to 40 per cent of all Japan's export earnings in the entire period from 1858 to the 1920s.

The Role of the State

Officials of the new Meiji government did not immediately recognize either the difficulties of industrialization or the extent of the domestic and international advantages their new nation enjoyed. Only by a process of trial and error were policies conducive to economic development put in place, and not infrequently what proved to be the most successful policies for stimulating development were motivated by other considerations. That said, however, it cannot be denied that the very commitment of those officials to Japan's economic transformation and the policies they ultimately hit upon to promote it were very important ingredients in the outcome.

The experience of China since the 1840s provided a negative example to the leaders of the Meiji government, and to their credit they paid heed to it. Scrupulous efforts were made to prevent attacks on foreigners or other incidents that might give Western governments cause to send punitive expeditions, exact reparations, or secure further treaty rights. The risks of foreign borrowing were perceived, as were the consequences of allowing Westerners to maintain and possibly extend their control over Japanese trade and shipping. Quickly persuaded of the superiority of Western military technology, Japan's leaders were determined not only to avoid military clashes with the West but also to equip their country with that same technology. Orders were placed in Britain for a few gunboats, and the handful of modern foundries, shipyards, and munition works inherited from the old regime were developed further, in the process giving a boost to general engineering within Japan.

If concern over national security played a role in the initiation of government policy toward the economy, however, it was soon to be matched by the government's pressing need for revenue and concern over internal security. The new Meiji regime had taken over the debts as well as the assets of the old regime, and the former, which included paying stipends to samurai throughout Japan after the abolition of the domains in 1871, were proving increasingly onerous. Although the government could now tax agriculture throughout the country, rather than just in former Tokugawa territories as at first, the payments it received were largely in kind, and their value fluctuated from year to year according to harvests and rice prices. In addition, the foreign trade surpluses Japan had enjoyed during the first few years after its reopening had given way to mounting deficits, as imports of Western yarns and textiles soared. When efforts by a Japanese mission to the West in 1871–3 to revise the 'unequal' treaties and gain tariff autonomy came to naught, the government concluded that it had no alternative but to reduce its fixed expenditures, secure a stable source of tax revenue, boost exports, and promote import-substitution industries.

These were not simple matters. Reducing fixed expenditure meant depriving hundreds of thousands of samurai of their annual stipends, and risking the wrath of the only well-armed members of society. Reform of agricultural taxes ran the risk of increasing the burden on farmers in some parts of the country and inciting protest. Boosting exports and establishing import-substitution industries involved substantial expenditure on new technology that seemed beyond the reach of private individuals and necessitated costly improvements in transportation and other forms of infrastructure.

As it turned out, the Meiji government was able to achieve all of these early objectives, although it endured a series of samurai rebellions, rural uprisings, and false starts in the process. Samurai stipends were commuted into lump sum payments of cash and long-term government bonds in 1876, in a stroke reducing recurrent government expenditure by over a third. A new agricultural tax based on the assessed value of farmland and payable in cash was put into effect between 1873 and the end of the decade. As anticipated, the new tax brought a welcome degree of stability to government income and provided a substantial annual sum—some 90 per cent of all tax revenues and 60 per cent of consolidated revenues in the late 1870s and early 1880s—that the government could spend as it saw fit.

Much of that income was spent on the creation and expansion of state services, including a conscript army and modern navy, but a portion was devoted to direct and indirect investment in the economy. Here there were false starts aplenty, and a tangled mixture of motivations at work. On the same mission to the West that had shown them that treaty revision was as yet impossible, leaders of the government had become aware that Western technological superiority extended far beyond weaponry. Not only were they awed by the railways, the speedy transmission of information by telegraph, the factories filled with complex machinery, the huge and to them unbelievably productive farms, and such imposing institutions of what came to be known as 'civilization and enlightenment' as banks, department stores, and universities; they also acquired the partially inaccurate but useful notion that most of these were of recent origin in the West and could be swiftly imported into Japan, to create the same powerful effects of enterprise and the same power of the state, if only sufficient cash could be mustered to pay for them.

Barely possessed of the cash and buoyed by their belief that Japan was only about a generation behind the West, the leaders of Japan began in the mid- to late 1870s a veritable frenzy of modern technology transfer, and the ends to be achieved as a result swiftly escalated in response to domestic political developments. Not only would exports be boosted and import-substitution achieved, but safe new careers would also be provided to former samurai of ordinary status as factory employees or as operators of large-scale, Western-style farms in frontier regions such as Hokkaido. Those samurai who had once possessed more substantial stipends would use their cash payments and bonds to invest in local banks or railways, and reap sufficient profits to ease their adjustment to the new *status quo*. An up-to-date communications and transportation network would not only facilitate commercial transactions and the movement of goods. If trouble arose from any quarter, the government would know of it almost immediately and could dispatch troops speedily to deal with the situation. The more trappings of Western-style civilization and enlightenment Japan could display, the more likely treaty revision would become.

State-of-the-art machinery for reeling silk, spinning cotton, and manufacturing woollens was imported by the government in the 1870s and either sold to private investors on favorable terms or put to use in factories operated by the government itself. Hundreds of Western technical experts were employed to set up this and other imported machinery and, not unimportantly, to train Japanese in its maintenance and use; others were hired to advise on Western farming methods. Scores of young Japanese were sent abroad to study the industrial arts, science, and administration.

Relatively few of these undertakings bore the immediate fruit the government appears to have expected. Not until imported silk-reeling machinery was simplified by local mechanics in the 1880s, to lower capital costs and make greater use of labor, did machine-reeling become profitable and begin to supplant traditional hand-reeling. Only by importing cheaper raw cotton and using large numbers of workers in round-the-clock operations did the domestic cotton-spinning industry begin, in the late 1880s, to compete first at home and then in the China market with its much larger Western rivals. The newly established woollen industry was heavily dependent on orders from the military for uniforms and blankets and remained uncompetitive with foreign imports until well after the turn of the century. Such government initiatives of the 1870s as the promotion of extensive farming and animal husbandry proved economic disasters almost immediately and had to be abandoned. It was its ability to sustain losses on the industries it operated, largely on grounds of national prestige and security, to make decisions about its spending without significant imput from other quarters until the inauguration of constitutional government in 1890, and to shift its priorities in the face of the hard lessons it was learning that enabled the government to contribute in positive ways to economic development.

Chief among these positive contributions was heavy government spending on, and encouragement of private investment in, the nation's infrastructure. Here the impact of what much later came to be known as 'late development effects' was much in evidence. Modern banking and insurance companies, communication and transportation networks, public utilities, and mass education had developed in the West in response to the needs of economic growth; with a model of the industrial future it sought to achieve in existence, Japan could create a number of institutions in advance of demand and enjoy their demonstrated benefits early in its industrialization.

The government began promoting a modern banking system in 1872 and established a central bank in the 1880s. Not only did modern banks introduce the joint-stock company and Western business methods to Japan, they also made it possible to aggregate the relatively small savings of individuals throughout the country into investment capital of a sufficient scale for new undertakings in the private sector. The first steps in creating a nationwide postal and telegraph system were taken early in the Meiji era. Although intended primarily to serve the strategic and administrative needs of government, the system was open to all who could afford to pay to use it and traffic by individuals and private enterprises rapidly increased, speeding the exchange of information throughout the country.

Relying on one of the very few foreign loans it was willing to risk before the 1890s and on British materials and engineering expertise, the government oversaw construction of the nation's first railway line in 1870–2 to link Tokyo with the nearby port of Yokohama. It appears that the Japanese sent to work on this project, and—at government insistence—to receive formal lessons from the Scottish engineers on site, took full advantage of the opportunity to transfer what they already knew of surveying and riparian engineering to this new endeavor. A few years later a second stretch of railway linking Ōtsu on Lake Biwa with Kyoto, and eventually with Osaka and the port of Kobe, was built entirely by the Japanese. Japan's railway age had begun, and despite the somewhat slow and fitful expansion of track and the continued need to rely on imported Western rails and rolling stock until the early 1900s, a means of greatly reducing overland transport costs was at hand.

The government also provided subsidies to shipping firms and shipbuilders in an effort to create a modern merchant fleet and wrest control of Japan's international and coastal trade from Western companies. Somewhat later it funded modest but beneficial improvements in public health, urban water supplies, and flood control. As noted earlier, it was active in creating a nationwide education system that, despite an increasing emphasis on the inculcation of patriotism at the elementary level, did much in time to increase the overall levels of literacy and basic technical competence among the people.

It will come as no surprise to students of economic development that all this activity usually cost more money than was available to the government in revenue in any given year. The additional expense of suppressing the Satsuma rebellion by disaffected former samurai in 1877—the most serious challenge to the new regime's existence—forced the government to issue even more paper currency, while the outflow of gold and silver to pay for escalating trade deficits meant that its currency issues had less and less backing in precious metal. That the many banks established earlier in the decade could issue banknotes with no backing in gold or silver and were doing so apace exacerbated the problems of currency depreciation and inflation. Rice prices doubled between 1877 and 1880 and the prices of many other commodities increased markedly. As the new land tax was now payable in cash, and as the government could not refuse its own paper, it had to cope with a steep decline in the purchasing power of its tax receipts.

Faced with imminent financial crisis and opposed to the idea of floating a large loan to London to tide them over, the government opted for drastic retrenchment. Matsukata Masayoshi, who became finance minister in 1881, took immediate steps to balance the budget and establish a sound currency. Unprofitable government factories, except for those deemed essential to national security, were sold off to private interests; new consumer taxes were levied on tobacco and rice wine, and a number of government expenditures were shifted to prefectural governments, who were instructed to raise local taxes to pay for their new obligations; the quantity of money in circulation was sharply reduced, and the depreciated paper currency issued earlier by both government and local banks was retired over a period of years and replaced by notes issued by a newly established central bank, the Bank of Japan, which was granted the sole right to issue paper currency; funds obtained from the sale of government factories were used to purchase silver to back the new currency, and the banking system itself was reorganized to provide greater coordination in financial affairs.

These initiatives, which served to rescue the government from insolvency and possible collapse, also produced a severe recession, known as the Matsukata deflation, which set the stage for the subsequent economic development of Japan. It is highly unlikely, of course, that Matsukata and his colleagues were fully in control of the economic forces they unleashed, but the net result was the implementation of a fairly coherent and enduring developmental strategy in which consumption by the majority of the population was constrained by taxation and the fledgling modern sector was given priority in access to bank loans, subsidies, and other forms of assistance from the state. Viewed from another perspective, resources in the form of taxes and savings were extracted from the old economy and used to nurture the new.

The deflation greatly intensified the redistribution of income and wealth that had begun with the reforms of the early Meiji era and concentrated both more firmly in the hands of individuals who might well use them for productive industrial investments in future. Farmers, who had seen their tax burdens reduced and incomes increased during the inflationary boom of the 1870s, suffered most of all as rice prices plummeted by 50 per cent in the early 1880s. Although reviled by Matsukata for having taken on 'luxurious habits', indulged in the consumption of 'luxury goods', and contributed thereby to trade deficits and the depletion of the nation's specie reserves,[3] most farmers had in reality only briefly enjoyed an opportunity to increase their standard of living. Now they were faced with declining incomes and an increased burden of national, prefectural, and consumption taxes. Many fell into debt, and some lost their land to wealthier neighbors, becoming tenant farmers on holdings they once had owned. A similar abrupt end to modest increases in living standards befell many artisans, craftsmen, and small traders as recession and higher taxation hit home. Only the stronger and more competitive businesses in the country, especially those with the connections and the capital to enable them to buy the enterprises the hard-pressed government was selling, emerged in better shape. Former warriors who depended on interest from their government bonds and who had been 'suddenly reduced to dire straits'[4] by inflation—much to the consternation of a government only recently victorious in armed confrontation with members of the same group—recovered at least some of their purchasing power.

From the mid-1880s the government left agriculture and traditional small-scale industry pretty much to the operation of market forces. Virtually none of its land tax revenue was invested in the agricultural sector. Instead, farmers were exhorted to adopt the best practices then in existence and to observe the time-honored virtues of diligence and frugality. Nor was much assistance, other than the encouragement of trade associations and efforts to improve quality standards, made available to the producers of traditional goods. Although it was now considerably less involved in the direct operation of factories than had been the case early in the Meiji era, the government remained intensely concerned with the modern sector and used its fiscal resources, as well as the substantial funds available to it from a flourishing postal savings system and the special-purpose banks it created toward the end of the century, to facilitate the development of large-scale private enterprises in such fields as merchant shipbuilding, the manufacture of steel, and the generation of electricity.

The Popular Response

Even allowing for the miscalculations that government officials made along the way, and the considerations of short-term electoral advantage that were to color some of their economic policies in later years, it is clear that the state played an important role in Japan's industrial transformation. That said, without the efforts and enterprise of the people, economic growth and structural change would have been even slower than they were in actuality and might well have reached one or another of the impasses familiar in the annals of development. It was the positive response of the people to new opportunities that the state only helped to shape, and at times their dogged determination, that enabled Japan to achieve the goal the state had articulated. Deferring consideration of labor until the next chapter, I will conclude this chapter with some observations about entrepreneurship.

Until the late 1960s, it was taken as axiomatic by both Japanese and Western scholars that Japan's economic development had occurred 'from above'. According to this assessment, just as the Restoration itself had been carried out by members of the warrior class, so too was the industrialization of the new nation. While a few former warriors in government created the framework for modern growth, the many former warriors out of government provided most of the entrepreneurial initiative, using their education, the administrative experience they had acquired in their domains, and the capital they received from the commutation of their stipends to establish modern banks and factories. In the process, they brought to modern economic activity a spirit of service to higher authority—formerly the domain, now the nation—and a denigration of private profit that were to characterize Japanese enterprise thereafter.

Subsequent empirical research has cast considerable doubt on this portrayal of the sources of entrepreneurial activity, and it now appears clear that the contributions of samurai were considerably less important than once surmised. Not only did wealthy commoners establish more banks than did samurai; probably as a reflection of their experience in commerce—an activity that warrior ideologues of the Tokugawa period regarded as despicable—they ran those banks more sensibly and, hence, more successfully. The same can be said of early experiments in modern industrial production. Government officials imported what often proved to be inappropriate technology and the former samurai appointed to manage government factories worried more about their own bureaucratic advancement than about demonstrating the virtues of new modes of production to the people—it is said, for example, that the only sure way that aspiring entrepreneurs from commoner ranks could find out about the inner workings of the government's model silk filature at Tomioka was by contacting the factory's cook.[5] Meanwhile, commoners devoted their attention to making goods by new and more productive means. As mentioned earlier, it was commoners who pioneered the adjustment of state-of-the-art Western technology to Japanese economic realities—for example, by using water power instead of expensive steam boilers and wood instead of steel in silk-reeling—and commoners who established the first profitable ventures in cotton-spinning, sugar-refining and modern paper production.

Less affluent commoners—the millions of owners of small businesses in the cities and rural districts of Japan—were also responsive to new opportunities, although in less dramatic ways. Many took advantage of improvements in transport to obtain raw materials at lower cost and expand the geographical extent of their sales of finished goods; while remaining sole proprietors of their enterprises, they adopted some features of modern accounting to separate business from household expenditure. Some reorganized traditional cottage industries into factory production, while others began producing such new items as matches, pencils, or Western-style umbrellas by cottage-industry means. Meanwhile, the inexperience of many members of the warrior class in practical business matters or farming doomed a large proportion of the new ventures they attempted to failure. Only as passive investors—a useful but far from quintessentially entrepreneurial activity—did some of them contribute to economic development.

What motivated entrepreneurial activity by individuals in the Meiji era remains an under-explored chapter of modern Japanese history. 'Service to the nation' certainly figures in the accounts of leading industrialists written in the early 1900s, but these claims must not be accepted uncritically. In Japan, as elsewhere, it was what industrialists did, not what they or their official biographers said, that counts, and in their doings there is plenty of evidence of fascination with the intricacies of modern technology, cool calculation of self-interest, and the desire to accumulate wealth for the personal power and leverage it would confer. For the great majority of more ordinary entrepreneurs, of course, few published sources exist and their business records, to the extent they survive, lie moldering in local archives. It is probably not reckless to conjecture, however, that they felt liberated by the Meiji Restoration and the lifting of restrictions on their personal and occupational mobility. Encountering—and in some cases inventing—new opportunities, they set about seeking to improve their lives and the lives of their families.

4

Protest from Below

Shortly before noon on 1 September 1923 a massive earthquake struck Japan. Measuring 7.9 on the Richter scale, its epicenter was some 50 miles from Tokyo, the nation's capital. Over 100,000 deaths were reported there and in nearby Yokohama, the majority of them caused by the fires that were ignited by scattered embers from overturned charcoal cooking stoves and that spread rapidly through the many wooden buildings in both cities. In the days following the earthquake, several thousand Korean residents were killed by angry mobs reacting to rumors—unfounded, it later turned out—that Koreans were engaging in arson and poisoning wells. Subsequently the military police arrested and killed several Japanese labor union activists, the anarchist Ōsugi Sakae, his mistress (and active feminist) Itō Noe, and Ōsugi's 6-year-old nephew. Well over half of all the buildings in Tokyo and Yokohama were destroyed, and six prefectures in the Kantō plain and surrounding areas, home to almost 20 per cent of the total population of Japan at that time, were declared disaster areas. The economy reeled from the loss, virtually overnight, of some one-eighth of Japan's total wealth. Millions were left homeless.

The greatest natural disaster to date in modern Japanese history, the Great Kantō Earthquake also became a symbol of the decade or so following the First World War to a later generation of Japanese scholars. Just as the land mass of Japan was thrown into violent upheaval by the action of plate tectonics deep beneath the sea, so too did Japanese society appear to be in turmoil, its very fabric strained by conflict on an unprecedented scale. The analogy may have been somewhat overdrawn, but it was fundamentally appropriate. Although there had been conflict earlier, it had occurred infrequently and involved relatively few people. The situation began to change in September 1905, when angry crowds rioted for three days in Tokyo after the police intervened to ban a public rally in Hibiya Park against the terms of the treaty bringing the Russo-Japanese War to an end. At least seven large-scale riots occurred in the capital during the following twelve years, triggered by public opposition to such diverse issues as increases in tram fares, political corruption, and national policy toward China.[1] By the mid-1920s many Japanese, in many parts of the country, either were engaging directly in collective protest against some basic aspect of the *status quo* or were expressing their discontent, and their heightened aspirations, in more oblique ways.

The Rice Riots of 1918 marked a watershed in the annals of popular discontent, not only in their eventual scale but also in their place of origin, deep within Japan's hinterland. Reacting to the quadrupling of rice prices during the wartime boom years and to evidence of hoarding by rice dealers, fishermen's wives in Toyama Prefecture launched the first in a series of demonstrations which spread over the next eight weeks to forty-two of Japan's forty-seven prefectures and may have brought as many as two million people onto the streets in one form of protest or another. Soon thereafter, the number of unions formed by workers in factories and by tenant farmers in the countryside began to multiply, and strike action by both factory workers and tenant farmers increased. While a small band of suffragettes lobbied unsuccessfully for the right to vote, many of the women at work as operatives in textile factories and—a more recent development—as secretarial staff in companies were becoming exasperated not only with poor working conditions and low pay, but also with the expectation that they would give most of their paychecks to their parents. Some younger women began spending more of the money they earned on themselves, and the most defiant among them had their hair cut short and began to patronize the coffee houses and dance clubs of urban Japan. A substantial share of the bright young men who had achieved admission to the élite higher schools and universities of Japan began to attend Marxist study groups, and some among them took part in 'to the people' campaigns in the early 1920s to raise the political consciousness of the masses. A national organization, the Suiheisha, was formed in 1922 to press for an end to social discrimination against the *burakumin*, Japan's outcast class. Residents of cities other than Tokyo took part in organized protests against the high costs of public transport, rented housing, and electricity, as well as corruption in urban politics. Later in the decade, and on into the 1930s, there was an upswing in the membership of civilian and military nationalist societies, some of them calling for a more active foreign policy and others agitating for radical economic and political reform at home.

To the observer of development today, at least some of these manifestations of restiveness and assertiveness among the people might well be seen in a positive light, as signs of a growing consciousness of citizenship and of nascent demands from below for democratization of the system. That is not how the situation was viewed at the time, however, by the most powerful members of the Japanese political and economic establishment. They were alarmed by popular unrest. The very 'evils' of industrialization that Meiji bureaucrats had hoped to avoid by the timely application of social policies now loomed before them, and the threat they sensed was heightened by the specter of the ongoing Russian Revolution. As we shall see, officials intervened actively to prevent what most of them saw as a potentially very dangerous situation from getting out of hand. First, however, we need to take a closer—and more dispassionate— look at the phenomena to which they were reacting, beginning with a brief foray into demographic and employment trends. Rather than attempting to account for every aspect of unrest during this period, I will focus on the upwelling of discontent among tenant farmers and industrial workers. Much of what I have to say, however, especially about the empowering consequences of education, applies to other sectors of the population as well.

Demographic and Employment Trends

The population of Japan had grown from about 35 million in 1872 to 55 million in 1920, the year of the first modern census; by 1935 the population had increased to 69 million. Although a few hundred thousand Japanese had emigrated to the United States and Brazil and perhaps 2 million others had managed to carve out a niche for themselves in Japan's colonial empire in Asia, the great bulk of this population increase had been accommodated at home, in urban or urbanizing areas. Although the absolute number of farm households remained virtually unchanged, the proportion of the population living in small, predominantly rural administrative districts with fewer than 10,000 residents declined from 87 per cent in the late 1880s to 54 per cent in the mid-1930s. In 1925, close to 13 million people, or 21 per cent of the total population, lived in cities, of which there were 101 nationwide; in 1935, over 22.5 million people, some 32 per cent of the total population, lived in cities, of which there were now 127.[2]

Only a relatively small portion of urban population growth up to the mid-1920s was the product of natural increase among town and city residents; most of it came from social movement, or migration. Large numbers of people, mostly young in years, had moved from villages to urban areas, or to the country places where many non-agricultural enterprises were located in the Meiji era and that grew fairly steadily thereafter into towns or even cities. This does not appear to have been either a random or a particularly stressful process as far as the migrants themselves were concerned. Rather than the flooding of a few central cities with desperate, illiterate, and unskilled rustics—the stereotypical and rather problematic image of urban population growth in an industrializing country—Japan's internal migration was, on the whole, the measured product of both 'push' and 'pull' factors, and relatively few migrants found themselves that far from home or in an environment for which they were totally unprepared.

It was the surplus natural increase of the countryside—the younger sons of farm families for whom there was no secure place in agriculture, because most farms were already too small to be subdivided further, and the teenage daughters of farm families who could earn useful cash for their fathers in the years before they married into other families—that left for residence and employment elsewhere, and in most cases the way of these young migrants was smoothed, as it had been during the Tokugawa period, by parental action. These 'surplus' children had been raised with the expectation that they would leave home eventually, and fathers were supposed to take what steps they could to secure places for them. In contrast to the past, and especially from the 1890s when the pace of economic growth quickened, the potential opportunities were greater, and not necessarily very far away. Daughters were much sought after by recruiters for the burgeoning raw silk industry, most of whose filatures were located in the countryside, and there was work for non-inheriting sons on construction crews or as employees in shops and small workshops that might well be located in towns and cities in the same or an adjacent prefecture. Not infrequently, in the Meiji era at least, these sons went to work for a kinsman or for a local entrepreneur with whom their families had long had dealings, in a job not unconnected with the by-employments practiced in their home villages and for which they had some training; when they were older, a marriage with a girl from their home village would be arranged for each of them, and in time their sons might move on to an even larger town or city. More affluent rural families could provide their younger sons with higher education to qualify them for careers in business, teaching, or government service. This could well lead to a more distant, and possibly more wrenching, move away from home, but only a minority of younger sons traveled this route, and in most cases the social status and comfortable standard of living they thus acquired, as participants in the 'new' Japan, appear to have provided sufficient compensation.

Had the pace of expansion in non-agricultural employment opportunities been more rapid, or had males rather than females been preferred for work in silk filatures and cotton mills (as was the case, for example, in India), an absolute decrease in the agricultural population might well have occurred and an incentive thereby been provided for the development of more extensive, increasingly mechanized farming. As it was, farming remained organized as a family undertaking, highly dependent on human labor, with decision-making authority passing over time from the father to one of his sons and from the mother to that son's wife. In most rural communities the same families were in residence in the 1920s and 1930s as in the 1880s; only where new land could be reclaimed for farming had branch families of existing farm families been established, and only where a resident family had failed to secure a successor, by birth or by adoption, had it disappeared from the scene. Most families lived in the same houses from generation to generation, and as in the past neighboring families co-operated with one another in the exchange of labor and in observances of births, marriages, and funerals.

One must be careful not to exaggerate the consequences of these demographic trends. Rather than two radically different environments—the one rural, agricultural, and traditional in both technology and social relations; the other urban, industrial, and modern—a broad spectrum of environments had come into being by the early 1920s. Just as urban Japan ranged from the great cities of Tokyo and Osaka, with populations of 2.2 million and 1.8 million respectively, to some forty provincial cities with populations of under 50,000 and well over 1,000 towns with fewer than 30,000 inhabitants, so too did the villages of rural Japan vary in population size and density, proximity to towns and cities, cropping patterns, and occupational structure. Not everyone in every village was a farmer pure and simple; indeed, many village residents in some parts of the country spent much of their time in non-agricultural activities. Nor was the continuity in the families that resided in any village necessarily accompanied by continuity in the economic hierarchy they formed. Some families prospered, acquired more land, and/or became more involved in local commerce and manufacturing; others fell into debt and were forced to sell all or part of their land, in many cases becoming tenant farmers on fields they once had owned. During the Tokugawa period there had been a high degree of congruence between familial wealth and political power within most villages. Where that congruence was upset, or where those families that had long dominated village politics failed to respond to the changing needs and interests of other residents, tensions within the community and strains in long-established relationships among families could well develop.

It is important to emphasize, too, that very few of those who left the villages for towns and cities ended up straightaway in modern industrial or commercial employment. Granted, the number of persons working in manufacturing increased from slightly over 700,000 in the early 1870s to almost 4 million in 1913, but just as the unexamined use of these figures in some econometric analyses gives a false impression of the speed of Japan's economic transformation, so too it distorts the extent by which employment in this area actually changed. The vast majority of these 4 million worked in 'factories' with fewer than five employees, producing goods without the assistance of inanimate power or anything much in the way of machinery. Although the materials that a minority of them used or the goods that a minority of them produced were new to Japan, the technology and organization of production this minority experienced in the workplace were virtually identical to the technology and organization of production that prevailed in indigenous manufacturing. Much the same can be said of retail trade, construction, and—with a few notable exceptions, such as railways—domestic transport. Here, too, the number of gainfully employed persons increased dramatically during the Meiji era, but the kind of work most of these employees performed and the environment in which they performed it differed little from the past.

Because the quantitative information at our disposal for the years prior to 1914 was collected and classified by industry—by what was produced, not by what means—it is necessary to estimate the growth of new, more modern forms of employment. According to one of these estimates,[3] in the early 1880s only some 400,000 people out of a total non-agricultural workforce of roughly

7 million worked in the infant modern sector of the economy, and more than half of these people were employed by the government as officials, policemen, teachers, army and navy personnel, or workers in government arsenals and factories; fewer than 200,000 people were employed by modern private enterprises. By 1913, the non-agricultural labor force had expanded to roughly 14 million, but despite a quadrupling of employment in the modern sector (to roughly 1.6 million, including government services) almost 90 per cent of all employment outside farming remained in activities that had changed little—except in the sheer number of people involved in them—since the Restoration.

During these same years, and on into the early 1930s, well over half of those employed in modern factories—that is, factories that used some degree of Western or Western-style machinery and one form or another of inanimate power—were women and young girls. A reflection of the preponderance of textile production within the modern sector, this did not lead automatically to the stunting of proletarian consciousness that many observers of the time and since have assumed. The first strike in modern Japanese history was carried out by female silk-reelers in 1886, and working women thereafter in both silk filatures and cotton mills were far from passive in the face of workplace issues that concerned them. That said, the presence of many sojourners within the female work force, who expected to leave factory employment for marriage after a few years and who were thus inclined to endure rather than try to change what they found uncongenial about their employment, the isolated locations of many factories employing women (with the important exception of cotton mills, which were located in coastal cities), and the unskilled or semi-skilled work that most of these textile workers performed, combined to make them followers, rather than leaders, in labor militancy during the 1920s.

At any rate, it was a mushrooming of employment opportunities for males in modern factories during the early 1900s, and especially during the boom years of the First World War, that was to prove most immediately relevant to the upsurge in labor unrest thereafter. These male workers were distinguished from most of their female counterparts by the more highly skilled labor they were expected to perform (or, at the very least, the greater physical strength they needed on the job), their longer term commitment to working for a living, and, in many cases, their status as the sole or chief wage earner in their families.

Confining our attention for the moment to factories with five or more workers—a crude indication of industrial modernity, to be sure, but one that is often used—the number of employees rose from roughly 800,000 in 1909, of whom about 300,000 were men, to over 1.6 million in 1920, of whom some 740,000 were men. Men began to outnumber women in factory employment in the early 1930s, and by the late 1930s there were some 1.7 million men in a much-expanded factory labor force of 2.9 million.

One of the most striking features of this same period was the growth in the number of factories employing 100 or more workers. In 1909, there had been slightly over 1,000 such factories; by 1920, there were over 2,000; and by the late 1930s, over 4,000. Although they formed only a tiny fraction of all manufacturing enterprises in the country—even in 1940 there were still more than 550,000 manufacturing workshops with fewer than five employees, and more than 132,000 factories with from five to ninety-nine employees—these larger enterprises very swiftly began to account for the majority of all modern industrial employment. In 1909, their combined workforces had totaled 345,000, or 42 per cent of all employees in factories with five or more workers. By 1920 their combined workforces totaled 946,000, or 53.8 per cent of all such employees. Of these 946,000 workers, 382,000—40 per cent of those in factories with 100 or more workers and almost 22 per cent of all those employed in factories with five or more workers—were employed in enterprises with 1,000 or more workers.

Among these larger factories were a number of textile firms—bastions of light manufacturing and the employment of women—but a substantial and growing number were engaged in the production of metals, machinery, and chemicals. This was heavy industry, where the very nature of the processes of producing such items as steel, locomotives, or inorganic fertilizers required larger units of operation and considerable investment in technology and machinery. Like cotton mills, most of these larger factories were located in or on the fringes of major coastal cities, close to the sources of the imported raw materials many of them required and to outlets at home and abroad for the sale of the goods they produced. Unlike cotton mills, these larger factories were employers of men, and most of the men they hired were skilled workers. By the early 1900s these men formed a small but increasingly self-conscious and vocal labor aristocracy. Better paid than textile operatives and unskilled male laborers, they felt they had raised themselves a cut above the great majority of urban workers, and they were sensitive to any threat to their position. It was no coincidence that labor unrest increased as the number of skilled male workers in heavy industry increased during succeeding years.

The Origins and Extent of Labor and Tenant-Farmer Protest

In Japan, as elsewhere, it was not the most downtrodden and desperate among industrial workers who took part in strikes and other action to improve pay and conditions, but the most highly skilled and best paid among them. Much the same can be said of tenant protest, which was concentrated during the 1920s in districts with lower than average tenant rents and higher than average involvement in the commercial market-place by tenant cultivators as well as landowners. Nor was tenant protest directly inspired by labor protest, as some at the time and since have argued. There were connections between the two movements, to be sure, but on the whole each developed independently, at roughly the same time and for broadly the same reasons. Let us deal with each of these points in turn, beginning with the last.

Of key importance in engendering the desire and the ability to challenge the *status quo* among both industrial workers and tenant farmers were basic education and military service. With every passing year, the population of Japan became not only proportionately younger than in the past, but also better educated. By

1910, the overwhelming majority of all Japanese children were attending elementary school for what had become in 1907 a statutory period of six years. While there was, as noted earlier, a substantial patriotic thrust to the instruction they received, there was an equal, and probably greater, emphasis on basic literacy and numeracy. Not all children acquired these basic skills to the same extent, of course, but on the whole they gained a degree of facility in reading, writing, and doing sums well beyond what might have been expected of their parents and most certainly of their grandparents. Granted, the sons of the urban and rural poor were far less likely to go on to higher education than were the sons of better-off families, because of the costs involved for tuition and maintenance, but even with an elementary education only, their horizons had been broadened and their ability to acquire new knowledge on their own enhanced. It is suggestive of a wider trend, I suspect, that a survey of 344 working-class households in Tokyo in 1912 found that 238 of them took a daily newspaper, as well as weekly and monthly magazines.[4] That the texts in many publications of the time were provided with *furigana*, which gave the phonetic readings of all the ideographs used, meant that even those who knew hardly any of the thousands of ideographs used in written Japanese could understand them.

Although it was not until the early 1920s—when the cohort of 6-year-old children in 1910 had reached young adulthood—that the full impact of mass literacy was to be felt in both urban and rural Japan, it is worth noting that the written word began functioning occasionally as a tool of organization and protest around the turn of the century. For example, tenant farmers in Shimane Prefecture drafted detailed by-laws for the union they established in 1896. One of the leaders of the successful strike by railway engineers that shut down the Japan Railway Company's Tōhoku line from Tokyo to Aomori in 1898 published an account of the strike's aims soon thereafter, and written statements of grievances, for submission to management and to the press, were not unusuadl in the other strikes of this period. *Yūai shinpō*, the monthly (later, twice-monthly) publication of the Yūaikai, a friendly society founded in 1912 by the social reformer Suzuki

Bunji, invited contributions from readers to its new correspondence section in 1914, and factory workers responded with a stream of observations and complaints.

Nor should we ignore the potentially destabilizing effects of the patriotic instruction young Japanese received from the mid-Meiji period onward. There were homilies aplenty on diligence, frugality, and filial piety in the ethics classes that every youngster attended, but there was also celebration of the emperor and his benevolent concern for each and every one of his subjects. Acceptance of this portrayal of the monarchy could inspire gratitude and humility, as was intended by the Ministry of Education, but it could also produce indignation, when those exposed to it subsequently became aware of a seeming gap between theory and practice. If the emperor's benevolence extended to one and all like the rays of the risen sun, then why did many of his subjects inhabit the shadows of poverty and deprivation? This question was to figure prominently in the language of discontent in the 1920s, and the answer which struck a resonant chord among many of the discontented—that landlords, factory owners, or others in positions of authority were impeding the emperor's wishes for his subjects—was to serve as a powerful justification for protest.

Military service intensified the impact of basic education on many young Japanese males. The Imperial Japanese Army had functioned since its inception in the early Meiji era as a potent instrument of social change so far as ordinary soldiers were concerned. Not only did the army introduce conscripts to trousers, jackets, and boots as well as to biscuits, beer, and beef, it also trained them in discipline and co-ordinated action. Perhaps most importantly, in terms of the present discussion, it did so in an environment in which their social origins counted for nothing. What mattered was what the conscripts themselves could do, not the status of their families, and they were rewarded, or punished, according to their own achievements. This differed from the civilian world that the sons of tenant farmers and factory workers had known, where one was expected to bow before those of superior wealth and social station and use humble speech in addressing them. Many of them found army life a liberating experience for this very reason, and the memory of it influenced their aspirations and behavior in later years.

It should be noted that the bows and humble speech referred to above were not rituals to be performed only on rare occasions of high significance, as is the case for most of us in the developed world today, but an integral part of daily life. Although the equality of all Japanese had been proclaimed in the immediate aftermath of the Restoration and new opportunities for social mobility came into being soon thereafter, there was no sudden revolution in social relations. The assumption that men of wealth and position were morally superior to those of lower status continued to prevail. By virtue of their lack of property and their dependence on others for their livelihoods, tenant farmers and factory workers were base, and the worlds they inhabited were structured by tangible reminders of that fact.

Tenants were expected to step aside if they encountered anyone of superior status on a village road or footpath. They were at the beck and call of their landlords, to perform chores in the landlords' fields or in the landlords' homes, even if this meant delaying vital chores of their own. If they were given a meal at the end of their day's labor, they received it gratefully and consumed it in a dark corner of the landlord's kitchen. If they encountered difficulty in paying their rents, which (unlike land taxes) were still due in kind, they were expected to approach their landlords individually, appearing meekly at their doors, to request relief. Similarly, manual workers in modern industry were required to enter factories through the special gates set aside for them, and were in many cases subjected to body searches when they left for home. There were separate canteens and separate toilets for workers, clerks, and managers. Workers were excluded from the benefits such as company housing, profit-sharing bonuses, and health care that some large enterprises began providing to their managerial and, to a lesser extent, their clerical personnel in the late 1890s. If workers experienced difficulty in stretching their wages to cover their expenses, they were expected to petition management for the favor of an increase in pay. As in the countryside, they were required to abase themselves, literally and linguistically, before anyone of superior status, while their superiors addressed them by their surnames alone, without the polite suffix *san*. Not infrequently, factory foremen and workshop supervisors used their considerable influence over hiring, work assignments, and promotions to extract kickbacks, gifts, or cash bribes from workers.

It would have been an unusual development in the annals of modern history had those who enjoyed the tangible and intangible perquisites of superior status decided spontaneously to treat their underlings differently. In Japan, as elsewhere, much of the pressure for this came from below, from the underlings themselves. Increasingly aware of their own competence, tenant farmers and industrial workers began to grumble about the demeaning treatment they received and to resent the submissive behavior that was expected of them. They might be poor, but they too were human beings. It was unjust for landlords, who 'spent their days in idleness',[5] or supervisory personnel, who might have academic credentials but lacked 'seasoned practical skills',[6] to treat them like scum. After all, they were producers, and the labor they performed was important to the nation, as well as to those who employed them. As one tenant union leader put it in the early 1920s, in the past we thought that 'our existence depended on the grace and favor of landlords'; now we realize that it is 'our labor that enables landlords to live'.[7] 'The majority of Japanese are farmers, and the majority of farmers are tenants', wrote another union leader. 'By their efforts the nation is protected, its land cultivated, and its people fed.'[8]

Not all tenant farmers or all factory workers came to this reassessment of their role and worth at precisely the same moment or with precisely the same degree of intensity. The misgivings and resentments engendered by elementary education and conscription may have been widespread, but it took the rather abrupt changes in economic circumstances that some tenant farmers and some factory workers experienced in the late 1910s and early 1920s to galvanize their private feelings into concerted action aimed at reforming the *status quo*.

The vast majority of tenant farmers paid their landlords an agreed volume of the harvest, not an agreed percentage, and this meant that if tenants succeeded in raising yields on the land they cultivated they would end up with more produce to consume and/or sell. This is precisely what happened, but it did not happen everywhere in the country at the same pace. If one considers only the nationwide statistics on agriculture, one sees a slow but fairly steady increase in the output of rice and other major crops between the 1880s and the early 1920s, an exceedingly slight increase in the level of rents paid by tenants during the same period, and, as a result, a substantial increase over time in the volume of harvests remaining in tenant hands. These aggregated national statistics mask considerable regional differences, however, and provide an unreliable guide to what was actually happening in the countryside.

At the very least, it is essential to disaggregate the national average into two very differing regions. In one of them, which we might term the heartland of Japan—those districts within the ambit of Osaka in the central south-west of the archipelago and Edo/Tokyo in the central north-east—output levels had been higher than elsewhere during the latter years of the Tokugawa period. It was here, especially in the south-west, that a variety of relatively low-cost methods of improving agricultural productivity had been invented during the nineteenth century, and here that these methods had been most assiduously exploited by local farmers, including tenant farmers, in the years following the Restoration. By the early 1910s, however, essentially all of the gains achievable by these means had been realized, so far as rice and other major crops were concerned. In the other region, which we might term the periphery of Japan, a harsher climate, the small size of most castle towns, and/or the difficulties of transporting produce beyond domain boundaries had contributed to relatively low levels of agricultural output during the Tokugawa period. The improved techniques of the heartland spread to the periphery after the Restoration, but the process of diffusion was slow, and even in the 1920s scope remained for the achievement of further gains in output by the fairly simple and inexpensive means pioneered elsewhere.

While tenant farmers in the periphery continued to benefit to an extent from increases in output, tenant farmers in the heartland faced an impasse. Unable, as in the past, to wrest gains from the land itself, their attention focused increasingly on the rents they paid their landlords: if these could be lowered, they would be better off. It was here, in the heartland, that tenant unrest was concentrated in the 1920s and that collective action by hitherto deferential 'underlings' sent shockwaves through the establishment.

Once again, it is essential to disaggregate the statistics. Nationwide figures reveal what some might regard (mistakenly, in my view) as a fairly modest level of rural discontent in the years between 1917 and 1930. In no single year during this slightly elongated decade did disputes involve more than 4 per cent of the nation's 3.8 million tenant-farming households. When one focuses on the heartland, however, a radically different picture emerges.

Of the 21,569 disputes reported between 1917 and 1930, over 16,000 (some 74 per cent of the total) took place in only nineteen of the nation's forty-seven prefectures, and these nineteen formed a virtually contiguous block from Niigata, Saitama, and Kanagawa in the central north-east to Osaka, Mie, Nara, and Wakayama, and thence along both sides of the Inland Sea to Fukuoka in northern Kyushu (see *Fig.* 1). Of the 1,144,418 tenants who took part in disputes between 1920 (the first year for which data on the number of participants are available) and 1930, fully 78 per cent lived in these same nineteen prefectures, which collectively contained less than 45 per cent of the nation's tenant-farming population.

Similar discrimination is required in dealing with statistics on industrial labor disputes. In no single year during the period 1917 to 1930 was more than about 5 per cent of the industrial labor force involved in strikes, lockouts, or slowdowns. But here, too, the incidence of unrest was skewed. As a general rule, the larger and more capital-intensive the enterprise and the more masculine its workforce, the more pronounced the unrest.

Industry was, of course, more diverse than agriculture and subject to a greater variety of exogenous forces, but even by the

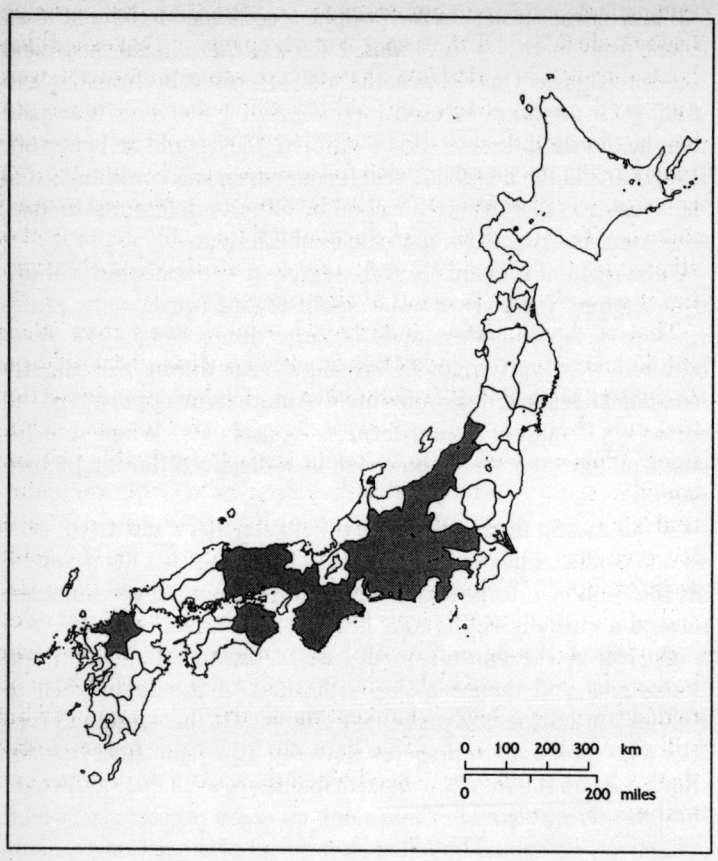

Fig. 1. Geographical concentration of tenancy disputes, 1917–1930 (based on data in Nōrinshō, Nōmukyoku, *Kosaku nenpō*, 1931). Shaded areas indicate the nineteen prefectures in the 'heartland' of Japan, where some 74% of all reported disputes took place.

same crude measure used above, the skewing of unrest is clear. Of the 5,592 industrial strikes and lockouts recorded between 1917 and 1930, 3,797, or 69 per cent, took place in manufacturing industries, with the remainder spread unevenly among the mining, transport, communications, construction, gas, and electricity industries. Of the 723,338 participants in strikes and lockouts during this period, over 511,000, or some 70 per cent, were employed in manufacturing. Within the manufacturing sector itself, over half of all strikers came from the minority of workers (no more than 30 per cent of all those employed in manufacturing concerns with five or more workers) who were employed in heavy industry. Textile workers, who accounted for some 55 per cent of all employees in manufacturing, ranked a distant but not insignificant second, at 33 per cent of all strikers.

That workers in heavy industry were more likely than others within manufacturing industries or within the industrial sector as a whole to engage in strikes should not be taken as an indication that only they were unhappy with their pay and working conditions. What enabled them to begin striking for better pay and conditions at a rate far greater than their numbers in the industrial labor force might suggest was the disproportionate degree of leverage they enjoyed *vis-à-vis* their employers during the boom years of the First World War, when expansion both in plant size and in the number of plants in heavy industry had intensified competition among enterprises for workers with the requisite basic skills and created labor shortages that workers could exploit to their own advantage. What kept them striking at a reduced but still significant rate thereafter were the insecurity and job losses that many of them experienced when that boom came to an end in the early 1920s.

Responses to Unrest

To the small number of urban intellectuals who were hoping to achieve a socialist revolution in Japan during the 1920s, increasing strike activity by tenant farmers and industrial workers was taken as a sign of proletarian awakening. Objective conditions now mandated that they swing into action as a vanguard force to reshape the inchoate grievances of peasants and workers into a class-conscious political movement. For a variety of reasons, however—not least, the disagreements among left-wing intellectuals themselves over the fine points of Marxist theory and the rivalry among some of them for leadership of the movement—their efforts came to naught. Rather than blaming themselves for failing to find an effective means of communicating with and mobilizing peasants and workers, they blamed the 'proletariat' for its narrow and unyielding concern with such economic issues as rents and wages, and the state for its harsh suppression of their efforts.

One still finds echoes of this assessment in much of the secondary literature on the tenant and labor movements in Japan, but in my view, these analyses misconstrue the situation. While tenant farmers and industrial workers undoubtedly were concerned with rents and wages, both groups possessed—and, in the course of conflict during the 1920s, continued to develop—a broader agenda that transcended purely short-term economic objectives. Had their grievances been dismissed by those in positions of authority and left to fester, tenants and industrial workers might well have become convinced that only radical political change would meet their needs. Neither dismissal nor festering was allowed to occur, however, or at least not in sufficient degree to achieve the result that left-wing intellectuals desired. Like these intellectuals, the state was sensitive to the 'lessons' of recent history in other countries. Unlike them, it was in a position to benefit from an early, indeed from what might be seen as a premature, response to evidence within Japan of the discontents that had led to the polarization of society and to radical working-class political movements elsewhere. Suppression of left-wing activists was only the first, and not necessarily the most important, of a series of countermeasures the state employed to defuse what, by its lights, were dangerous trends.

For tenant farmers in the heartland during the 1920s, rent levels were both a basic matter that affected their livelihoods in any given year and an issue they could exploit to achieve further and longer lasting gains. Custom dating back to the Tokugawa period dictated that landlords reduce rents when crops were poor, just as daimyo were expected to reduce land taxes out of their benevolent concern for the villages within their domains. By the 1920s, the daimyo were long gone, but landlords remained vulnerable to the claims of concern for those who cultivated their land. As a pithy phrase of the time put it: 'In tenancy, poor harvests pay off.'[9] Far from being an expression of neurosis bordering on masochism among tenant farmers, this was an expression of perceived opportunity. By inducing their landlords' benevolence whenever yields fell noticeably below normal, they could begin an assault on the conditions of tenancy themselves and, eventually, on the power structure of their communities. This is what many tenants proceeded to do—to the dismay of left-wing intellectuals, because tenants were demonstrating more interest in local than national or international affairs.

Not only did the demands of tenants for temporary rent reductions tend to escalate into demands for permanent rent reductions and the involvement of tenant farmers in determining what fair levels of rent would be, but tenants also began to insist that their expertise and interests be taken into consideration in planning agricultural improvements within their communities and to organize co-operatives and other mutual assistance groups to provide for themselves some of the services for which they had formerly depended on their landlords, usually to the latters' profit. This was no mere economy measure, but part of a deliberate attempt by tenant farmers to seize control of their lives. What may have begun as a response to the ending of *de facto* rent reductions by means of increases in output became, in fairly short order, an assault on dependence and deference.

One can discern the existence of an equally extended agenda among skilled industrial workers. Wage levels were certainly an issue in strikes and other action during the hyper-inflationary years of the war, as was the level of separation payments for redundant workers when the boom came to an end in the early 1920s and many large firms decided to rationalize their operations. What is noteworthy, however, is the prevalence of efforts by workers in these years to bring an end to the real and perceived discrimination they experienced at the hands of their employers. Some pressed for the abolition of body searches at the factory gate and of the special uniforms, caps, and insignia that marked them as shop-floor workers; others demanded benefits, such as bonuses and pensions, that had been reserved previously for white-collar employees, and regular, predictable increases in wages (to eliminate favoritism on the part of foremen as well as the widespread practice on the part of factory managers of cutting the rates of pay for particular jobs to induce higher output). Although most of these efforts ended in failure at the time, they nonetheless constituted a rejection of subservience by industrial workers that was to figure prominently in the restructuring of personnel policies within large factories in the years ahead and lead, eventually, to the creation of what has become known as the Japanese employment system.

As noted earlier, the Japanese state was in a position to monitor trends in popular thought and behavior down to the rice-roots level of Japanese society and, given its inclination to protect Japan from the 'evils' of development, it was willing to act on its findings. While there were some among bureaucrats and politicians in the early 1920s who accepted social conflict of the sort they were witnessing as a pathway to progress, they were outnumbered—and ultimately outmaneuvered—by those who did not.

For convenience, we may divide the countermeasures adopted by the state into three categories: prophylaxis, pre-emption, and propaganda. To prevent the spread of revolutionary ideology from a coterie of intellectuals to the putatively healthy and innocent masses, left-wing activists were removed—first by harassment and eventually by arrest and detention—from contact with tenant farmers and factory workers; newspapers were discouraged from reporting details of tenancy disputes and industrial strikes, so as to prevent knowledge of the avenues of protest that others had pioneered from spreading to those as yet untainted by 'dangerous ideas'. The state then took steps to articulate some of the grievances of tenant farmers and industrial workers as its own and to provide a controlled degree of rectification. While avoiding formal recognition of their right to organize and bargain collectively (a step to which most landlords and industrialists objected strongly) the state established machinery for the mediation of disputes. Not unimportantly, it promulgated universal adult male suffrage in 1925, a measure which enabled tenant farmers in particular to gain a direct voice in the village and prefectural assemblies long dominated by local men of property. Last but not least, the state lobbied landlords and industrialists to consider the needs of those who depended on them for their livelihoods and to prevent disputes by timely concessions. This was part of a broader campaign the state had initiated not long before to 'revitalize' the virtues of harmony and consensus that were said to distinguish Japan from the harsher societies of the West. Consisting mostly of exhortation and slogans, this campaign emphasized that all must work together to build a strong and prosperous country. Conflict was not only unnecessary and wasteful; it was alien to the culture.

These official efforts did not lead to the immediate cessation of protest from below, but they did serve to check its uninhibited growth and to put those who engaged in it on the defensive. Dissent and assertiveness, as well as conflict itself, were deprived of the oxygen of legitimacy. If reform were needed, the state would provide it. As we shall see, it was not until after the Second World War that this increasingly strict orthodoxy would be challenged, at least for a time, by large numbers of ordinary Japanese.

5 | The Military in Politics

*D*uring most of the years between 1918 and 1932 the leader of one or another of the political parties in the lower, elected house of the Diet was appointed prime minister, formed a cabinet composed largely of his party colleagues, and, with them, governed the country. It seemed that the long-standing goal of political parties to realize 'normal constitutional government', by which they meant government led by the majority party in the Diet, had been achieved.[1]

The process of reaching that goal had been similar in many respects to the course of political development in Britain and the United States during the early decades of the previous century. In all three countries political parties had initially (and not totally without justification) been castigated by the wielders of political power as 'factions' representing narrow sectoral interests. They were perceived as a threat to the nation. Over the course of decades, by virtue of their skillful exploitation of parliamentary debate, the leverage they enjoyed as holders of the national purse-strings, and alliances with other strategic élites in politics and in society, parties had made themselves first useful and then indispensable to the functioning of national government. Finally they became the government.

A key difference, of course, was that party cabinets did not remain the norm in Japan. Although parties remained in existence throughout the 1930s, they lost possession of the cabinet in 1932. Thereafter Japan was governed by 'transcendental' or 'national unity' cabinets, in which all (or most) political élites were represented. The Diet continued to meet and elections continued to be held, but the lower house had lost its central place in national politics.

There was no single reason for the demise of 'normal constitutional government'. As is usually the case, a variety of factors—some of them relating to the political parties themselves—came together, in the late 1920s and early 1930s, to undermine the tenuous precedent that had been achieved. One of the most potent of these factors was the Japanese military, that is, the Imperial Japanese Army and Navy.

Since the mid-1920s elements of both services had been engaged in covert and eventually overt assaults on the legitimacy of party rule. After 1932 their high commands began to acquire for themselves the central place in national politics once occupied by the lower house. Neither service was totally successful in what was, to party politicians, 'abnormal' constitutional government. Even Tōjō Hideki, general of the army and both prime minister and minister of war from October 1941 to July 1944, was forced to compromise with the bureaucracy, economic interests, the military services—and even with the Diet. He was by no means a dictator, nor were Japan's domestic and foreign policies determined exclusively by its military during the late 1930s and early 1940s. Nevertheless, the military enjoyed greater success than political parties in acquiring both power and legitimacy. As one scholar has observed, it enjoyed 'a degree of intervention that the armed forces of most countries could achieve only by means of a coup'.[2]

How and why had the military achieved this position? Explanations which focus on Japanese culture—on the legacy of the samurai or on the inherent appeals of *yamatodamashii* (the Japanese spirit)—do not shed sufficient light on the subject. For a satisfactory understanding, we must look to Japan's recent history, to real events and their real or perceived significance.

We need first to consider a facilitating factor, insufficient in itself as an explanation but important once the military became motivated to assert itself in politics. Like the political parties, the military in Japan had enjoyed its own set of constitutional advantages since 1890. Chief among these were those conferred by certain articles of the Imperial Japanese Constitution (also known as the Meiji Constitution).

Article 3: The Emperor is sacred and inviolable.

Article 11: The Emperor has the supreme command of the army and navy.

Article 12: The Emperor determines the organization and peace standing of the army and navy.

Article 55: The *respective* Ministers of State shall give their advice to the Emperor and be responsible for it [emphasis added].[3]

According to accepted interpretations of articles 3 and 55, the emperor was above politics; he was not responsible for policy, for if he was and if policy proved a failure, his inviolability would be jeopardized. Those who bore responsibility (as individuals, not collectively) were the 'respective' ministers of state. They enjoyed 'access to the throne' to present their advice to the emperor—that is, to articulate policy.

Because the emperor was supreme commander of the army and navy (article 11) and 'determined' the organization and peace standing of each service (article 12), it followed that those responsible for military policy were the minister of war (army), the minister of the navy, and the chiefs of the general staff of each service. This was known as the right of supreme command. Since 1890 these provisions had been interpreted to mean that each service had complete control over its own internal administration (the domain of the service ministers of state) and over the conduct of military operations in wartime (the domain of the general staffs). They were not subject to cabinet (or 'civilian') control in those areas.

Given the principle of individual responsibility to the emperor, no minister of state was subject constitutionally to cabinet or even prime ministerial control. Indeed, cabinet cohesiveness was a problem of all governments under the Meiji Constitution. In effect, they were coalitions whose survival depended on the personality and political acumen of the prime minister, a spirit of give-and-take among his cabinet colleagues, and (during the 1920s) on a degree of party discipline.

What gave the military a potential additional advantage in these cabinet coalitions, and hence in the formulation of government policy, was an administrative order put through by Prime Minister (and Restoration 'hero') Yamagata Aritomo in 1899. According to the order, only generals and admirals on the active duty list could be appointed war or navy minister.

It is important here to distinguish between intention and consequence. Yamagata's intention was decidedly not to lay the basis for military ascendancy in Japan. On the contrary, he had considerably less sinister motives in mind: to contribute to the professionalization of the military and to insure continued caution in foreign policy.

Although all leaders of the Meiji government came from the warrior class, from early on a division of labor between civilian and military affairs had operated, and it had become accepted that military affairs would be left to experts—that is, to trained and experienced officers. No friend of the early political parties, Yamagata had long sought to keep both services above the partisan fray, free of party-political 'contamination' and dedicated to the national interest. Thus a ban on political activity and public advocacy by officers and men had been imposed in the early 1880s, and reiterated in the Imperial Rescript to Soldiers and Sailors of 1882.

'The soldier and sailor should consider loyalty their essential duty,' the rescript ordained. 'Neither be led astray by current opinion nor meddle in politics.' Also enjoined were propriety, valor, faithfulness, righteousness, and simplicity. Those in inferior ranks were to pay their superiors due respect and to regard the orders they gave as issuing directly from the emperor. 'Except when official duty requires them to be strict and severe', superiors were to treat their inferiors with kindness and consideration, 'so that all grades may unite in their service to the Emperor'. The rescript went on to observe:

Ever since the ancient times valor has in our country been held in high esteem, and without it Our subjects would be unworthy of their name . . .

But there is true valor and false. To be incited by mere impetuosity to violent action cannot be called true valor. The soldier and sailor should have sound discrimination of right and wrong, cultivate self-possession, and form their plans with deliberation. . . . If you affect valor and act with violence, the world will in the end detest you and look upon you as wild beasts. . . .

Faithfulness implies the keeping of one's word, and righteousness the fulfillment of one's duty. If then you wish to be faithful and righteous in anything, you must carefully consider at the outset whether you can accomplish it or not. If you thoughtlessly agree to do something that is vague in its nature and bind yourself to unwise obligations, and then try to prove yourself faithful and righteous, you may find yourself in great straits from which there is no escape.

If you do not make simplicity your aim, you will become effeminate and frivolous and acquire fondness for luxurious and extravagant ways; you will finally grow selfish and sordid and sink to the last degree of baseness, so that neither loyalty nor valor will avail to save you from the contempt of the world.[4]

Yamagata was one of the few Japanese soldiers at the time, and for a long time subsequently, to have known defeat in battle. In 1863 he had taken part in Chōshū's shelling of American, French, and Dutch ships at Shimonoseki and had stood by impotently a short time later when American and French warships returned to demolish the Chōshū defenses. The experience had made him a champion of military readiness and a critic of blind reliance on force. Although a committed imperialist in later years, he recognized that gains could often be made at less risk by diplomacy than by war. It was his aim, then, to keep the military free of popular passions, that pernicious 'civilian' disease, so that it could be employed as an obedient servant of the state.

In the short term he was successful in his aim: Japan's army and navy acted only when instructed to do so, and the negotiated settlement to the Russo-Japanese War of 1904–5 that aroused much popular criticism was accepted by the armed services without demur. In the longer term, however, his administrative order gave the services the ability to exert great pressure on the prime minister and the cabinet as a whole.

That only high-ranking officers could become service ministers was not the problem. The crux was that they must be on active duty, subject to the chain of command. The chief of the general staff concerned could order a service minister to resign and all others of requisite rank to refuse appointment. As a result, the cabinet would be incomplete and would collapse. This weapon was not used until 1912, and as it turned out, the use proved counterproductive, in that it outraged the political parties in the Diet and fueled the movement they championed for normal constitutional government.

Significantly, the issue that led the army high command to act in this instance was defense planning, not the internal administration of the service or military operations *per se*. The army wanted the remaining two divisions of the four that had been 'promised' it in 1906, to prepare for the feared czarist war of revenge, but the prime minister favored fiscal retrenchment and the allocation of scarce resources to promotion of the domestic economy, a view shared by party politicians in the Diet. The army minister resigned when his demand to the cabinet was refused, and the general staff refused to nominate a successor. The prime minister was forced to resign.

The issue of defense planning—and more broadly, competing visions of national-security needs—were to loom large in future, leading not only to tension between 'civilians' and the military, but also to inter- and intra-service rivalry. Indeed, from about the mid-1920s there was a veritable explosion of political activity on the part of both services. Yamagata's strictures against 'meddling in politics', not to mention his stress on obeying one's superiors, had become dead letters.

In the first place, many high-ranking officers had party connections of an informal sort, and members of both services were engaged in active campaigns in the media and in public lecture tours, as well as in government circles, to win allies for their policies and their vision of national-security needs.

Secondly, and more dramatically, a series of acts of insubordination by junior and field-grade officers occurred both at home and abroad. In 1928 a small group of officers of the Kwantung

Army, a force created to patrol the railway corridor in Japan's leased territory on the Liaotung Peninsula, assassinated Chang Tso-lin, warlord of Manchuria, hoping (in vain, as it happened) for an opportunity to extend Japan's control over Manchuria as a whole. In September 1931, field-grade officers of the Kwantung Army engineered another incident in Manchuria, continually defied orders from Tokyo to localize the conflict, and eventually forced both the government and the army high command to permit the creation of the puppet state of Manchukuo. On 15 May 1932, a group of young naval officers assassinated Prime Minister Inukai Tsuyoshi. In July 1935, a lieutenant-colonel marched into the office of Major-General Nagata Tetsuzan, head of the army's military affairs bureau, and hacked Nagata to death with his sword. Finally, on 26 February 1936, some 1,400 troops led by a small band of junior army officers assassinated the finance minister, lord keeper of the privy seal, and the inspector general of military education. Narrowly failing in their attempt to kill the prime minister too, they seized the center of Tokyo and demanded the sweeping away of existing governmental institutions and the realization of direct rule by the emperor.

An event that played a crucial role in bringing about this explosion of activity, in all its diverse and disturbing forms, was the First World War. Japan had been asked by its ally Britain for a limited degree of assistance in the early months of the war, but for a variety of reasons the Japanese government decided that it made sense to declare war on the Central Powers instead. For Japan, the actual fighting was brief and the economic gains, especially from increased trade with Western colonies in Asia, were great. But there were to be problems nonetheless. Chief among these was the debate in Japan (as in other countries) in the early 1920s over the military significance of the conflict. This led most immediately to antagonisms that almost tore the Imperial Japanese Army apart.

Prior to the First World War there had been general consensus within the army on the three cardinal principles of its organization: a professional officer corps, a large standing army, and an active reserve. The emphasis very clearly was on manpower, on infantry and cavalry troops. In addition, it was universally believed in army circles that Japan had won the Sino-Japanese War of 1894–5 and the subsequent Russo-Japanese War of 1904–5 because the army had been able to mobilize troops in sufficient number and generate an aggressive combat spirit among them. Bold attack, continual pressure on the enemy—these qualities of spirit had led to victory. *Yamatodamashii* was the nation's best defense.

After the First World War, some officers began to question this orthodoxy. Especially within the war ministry, the concept of total war took hold. Echoing the assessment of many Western military observers, officers in the ministry argued that Germany's had been an economic, not a military defeat. Militarily, Germany's performance had been brilliant, proving the value of mechanized forces, but the home front had been unable to sustain the burden of producing all of the tanks, howitzers, and airplanes the military needed. Victory in future wars, they argued, would depend not only on the military itself, but also on the economic and spiritual resources of the nation.

These officers became convinced of the need to mechanize Japan's own army, but they found the government of the day unwilling to provide the funding they required. The newly ascendant parties were committed to domestic economic development and the new post-Versailles world order of peaceful economic expansion. Recognizing that it was impossible to maintain a large standing army and mechanize at the same time, the war ministry deactivated four divisions, demobilized 38,000 men, and used the savings to purchase (and later to produce at home) the modern weapons of war the nation now required.

Proponents of the older combat tradition, among them not a few young officers just out of the military academy, were horrified. In their view, a vile and dangerous materialism had swept over the ministry, putting the nation itself at risk. A war of words, and swords, ensued, in which the office of inspector general of military education became a conspicuous battleground. Those inspectors general who tried to introduce greater technical training into the curriculum of the military academy, or those elsewhere in the army high command who supported such initiatives, ran the risk of assassination. Despite opposition, however, mechanization proceeded apace. Only on the parade ground did the older tradition hold sway. There were found infantry and cavalry troops aplenty, a sight that led many Western observers to dismiss the Japanese army as a 'museum piece' unworthy of serious concern.

The difficulties of getting Diet approval for military spending proposals in the early 1920s also exacerbated long-standing rivalry between the army and the navy. Since the late nineteenth century Japan had faced two sets of strategic concerns: the protection of the nation's continental interests against other land powers, a task entrusted to the army; and the protection of the home islands and Japan's insular possessions against other sea powers, entrusted to the navy. So long as each service could obtain the funding it required to meet its appointed task, interservice rivalry was held in check, but when funding proposals met with resistance, as they did after the First World War, the services found themselves in competition for increasingly limited resources. That, in turn, impelled their respective high commands into politics and public advocacy, as each found it necessary to lobby more actively than ever before for what it considered essential provision.

There was also growing opposition within each service toward the political parties and party government in general. Underlying this opposition may have been a degree of impatience with pluralism, the essence of parliamentary process, but specific issues too were involved. As military critics saw it, successive party cabinets in the 1920s were putting the empire at risk by seeking to co-operate with the Western powers in dealing with China and resurgent Chinese nationalism. Their refusal to fund the army and navy 'properly' was weakening national security. The special interests the parties served, especially big business, were dividing the nation at a time when unity was essential. This opposition came to a head in 1930 over the issue of the London Naval Treaty.

It had been the goal of the Imperial Navy after the First World War to have 70 per cent of the naval strength of the United States, its chief maritime rival, so that Japan's superiority over the US

The Military in Politics

Pacific Fleet in Japan's home waters would be assured. At the Washington Conference of 1922, however, Japan's representatives agreed to a 10 : 10 : 6 ratio in battleships and aircraft carriers for the US, British, and Japanese navies, in exchange for an agreement among all three parties that (with the exception for Japan of its four home islands and for Britain of Australia and New Zealand) they would not establish new fortifications and naval bases or carry out anything more than routine maintenance on their existing fortifications and bases in the area east of Singapore and west of Hawaii.

There was some resentment in the Japanese navy at this outcome, but generally the treaty was accepted, and the navy concentrated on constructing the smaller ships and submarines that were not covered by its terms. When the United States became aware of this building program and started a program of its own in the late 1920s, a naval arms race loomed. Then the Great Depression struck, and both sides became willing to seek a new agreement.

At the negotiating table in London in 1930, the United States pressed for a 10 : 10 : 6 ratio between the American, British, and Japanese fleets in all categories of vessel. After much debate, a compromise was worked out whereby the new ratio would come into effect in 1936; until then, Japan was permitted 70 per cent. This was acceptable to Prime Minister Hamaguchi and, albeit reluctantly, to the navy ministry, but the navy's general staff was opposed, on the grounds that the compromise would irreparably damage national security. The general staff decided to 'report directly to the throne', that is, to exercise the right of supreme command and let the supreme commander, the emperor, know of its opposition. Moreover, it made its opposition public, charging the cabinet with violating the constitution and endangering the nation. Although it received considerable support from the press and from the opposition party, the general staff was eventually forced to accept the treaty, but not before exacting two concessions: officials in the navy ministry who had supported the compromise were to be removed from their posts, and the prime minister agreed to seek closer liaison with both the army and the navy general staffs in future.

For the moment, the cabinet had prevailed and the treaty was ratified, but any sense of relief its members felt was short-lived. Prime Minister Hamaguchi himself was soon to be mortally wounded by an assassin's bullet, and although the assassin in this case was a civilian, apparently acting alone, there was small comfort in that fact. By its concessions the government had given the navy, and by extension the army, a greater voice in policy-making. It had recognized, tacitly but no less potently, that the autonomy of the general staffs—their independence from cabinet control—extended well beyond military operations in wartime. Subsequent party cabinets, and the national unity cabinets that succeeded them in 1932, were to find it increasingly difficult to resist pressures from the army and navy high commands for policies the services favored.

Divisions within the army and navy over policy muted the impact of the military on government decision-making for a time. Not until 1933–4 were advocates of naval limitation within the navy shunted aside, in a reshuffling known as the Ōsumi purge, and positions of influence within both the ministry and the general staff monopolized by members of a so-called fleet faction that rejected the London Naval Treaty. Only in the aftermath of the abortive coup attempt led by young officers in February 1936 did the army high command achieve an effective degree of control over dissidents within its own ranks. Although inter-service rivalry continued to the end of the decade—and, indeed, on through the Second World War in the Pacific—it abated somewhat with the outbreak of armed conflict with China in 1937 and a renewed willingness on the part of the Diet to appropriate the funds each service demanded.

The China 'Incident' also brought about the creation of a high-level decision-making forum, later known as the Liaison Conference, in which the closer contact between the government and the general staffs that Hamaguchi had promised in 1930 was amply provided. Consisting of the leading government ministers on the one hand (the prime minister and foreign, war, and navy ministers; sometimes the finance minister) and the chiefs and vice-chiefs of the army and navy general staffs on the other, these conferences began as informal sessions held occasionally at the prime minister's official residence to co-ordinate policy at a time of crisis. In theory, but never in practice, the decisions of these meetings were subject to cabinet veto. In effect, they became the *de facto* center of policy-making. From July of 1941, the conferences took place at Imperial Headquarters, with greater numbers of officers in attendance; they occurred weekly, if not more frequently, the agendas prepared by the mid-echelon army and navy officers assigned to the meetings as secretaries.

The Liaison Conference was one of several supra-ministerial bodies created during the mid- to late 1930s (the Cabinet Information Office and the Cabinet Planning Agency being two others) which collectively represented a breaking away from established institutions and bureaucratic procedures. Military men occupied strategic positions in all of these bodies, at the lower levels where proposals were formulated and at the upper where they were agreed. As Japan's foreign-policy options narrowed, owing in no small measure to miscalculations made by both its military and civilian leaders, and as the conflict in which the country was engaged widened from an undeclared war with China to war against the Allies in 1941, the perceived need for streamlined and co-ordinated decision-making intensified. As a result, power steadily accrued to these new *ad hoc* bodies, and military influence within the state increased.

In this process, the Japanese people played only an indirect role. Despite successive extensions of the right to vote after the inauguration of an elected national assembly in 1890, culminating in the enactment of universal adult male suffrage in 1925, Japan had not become a political democracy. The nation's leaders were appointed by high-ranking advisers to the emperor, not elected by popular vote, although election results did of course influence who was appointed prime minister during the era of party cabinets. Even during that brief era, however, and much more consistently after it ended, politics and policy formulation remained an élitist affair, structured by competition for ascendancy among the institutions of a highly centralized state—the Diet, the bureaucracy, the military services—which had been created more or less equal by the Meiji Constitution. That said, the evidence available to us suggests that many ordinary Japanese, in both rural and urban areas of the country, welcomed the military's rise to greater prominence and power during the 1930s.

To the extent that this was indeed the case, it does not follow that the Japanese people were by nature warlike. Granted, most of them were proud of Japan's colonial empire and aware of the role of the army and navy in acquiring it by success in battle. These were major themes in the schooling they had received as children after 1895 and in the celebrations of Japan's achievements to which they were exposed as adults, and consequently rather difficult to ignore. Moreover, as discussed in Chapter 4, conscription had proved a liberating experience to many soldiers of relatively humble social origin, by exposing them to new forms of discipline and new merit-based criteria for advancement. That this left many of them with a largely positive attitude toward the army is undeniable, but at the same time the essentially domestic focus of their admiration should not be ignored. The military services—especially the army, because of the greater numbers who experienced its rigors and rewards—were seen as champions of the people as well as defenders of the state. This was a perception that each of the military services took pains in the 1920s and 1930s to cultivate, in order to buttress the material and spiritual resources of the nation deemed essential to total war.

Had it not been for the recurrent economic dislocations of the interwar era, culminating in the Wall Street crash of 1929 and the Great Depression, which destroyed many small businesses in Japan, cost many industrial workers their jobs, and deprived many farm households of the essential income they earned from raising silkworms, it is possible that Japan's political parties might eventually have earned respect as the people's champion, but this was not to be. By the early 1930s party government became associated not only with impasse or failure abroad, but also—and more importantly, so far as many ordinary Japanese were concerned—with impasse or failure at home. Only the military seemed aware of the problems the people faced in their daily lives, and it was increasingly to the military that the people looked for the solutions they hoped would bring them a better future. In this they were to be mightily disappointed, and from that disappointment arose a profound antipathy toward the military in the years after Japan's defeat in 1945.

6 Modernization and its Discontents

*I*t may be useful at this point to pause and consider Japanese thought about the modernization of their country. My focus here will not be on developments in politics, the economy, or society, but rather on what successive generations of Japanese have made of those developments and, in particular, on what they have at times found troubling about them.

Although hardly a year has gone by in the past century or so without some amount of attention to the subject, I will confine my attention to three fairly discrete periods when, it seems to me, the discourse about modernization became intense. These are: the 1880s and 1890s, when the issue was first discovered and debated by a 'new generation' of young Japanese who had reached maturity in the aftermath of the Meiji Restoration of 1868; the 1920s and 1930s, when what might be termed the intellectual foundations of the Second World War in the Pacific were laid, as consensus gradually was reached among some of the best and brightest Japanese on the need for a 'new cultural order' at home and throughout Asia; and the 1970s and 1980s, the era of *Nihonjinron*, or the debate about Japaneseness. After a brief, and necessarily selective, examination of each period, I will make some observations about the general character and significance of Japanese thought about modernization in the century under consideration. But first let me make a few comments about the discourse to which I have referred.

In terms of the modernization theory on which I was nurtured, at least for a time, in the 1960s, Japanese thought about modernization since the late nineteenth century has revolved around two analytically distinct issues: the relationship between modernization and westernization, and the relationship between modernity and tradition. In the early Meiji period these relationships posed no difficulty. Modernization and westernization were taken as equivalent; modernity and tradition, as diametrically opposed. 'Evil practices of the past shall be abandoned, and actions shall be based on international usage', proclaimed the Charter Oath of 1868, and '[k]nowledge shall be sought all over the world'. 'International' and the 'world' in that document meant the Western world, just as it was Western-style 'civilization and enlightenment' (*bunmei kaika*) that was called for in one of the major slogans of the day.

It was not long, however, before these assumptions began to be questioned in Japan, as indeed they were eventually throughout Asia and the non-Western world. What many observers have noted in studying twentieth-century nationalist and independence movements—the revival of interest in indigenous tradition and the search for ways of synthesizing and blending tradition and modernity—began to occur.

To be sure, late nineteenth-century Japan was not a Western colony, as were, for example, India and Indonesia. But in many respects Japan was a 'colony in spirit',[1] in the sense that its people too, especially its intellectuals, had come to look to 'the West' as a basic source of new values. A Japanese scholar, Yano Tōru of Kyoto University, has put the issue somewhat differently and more broadly. Borrowing the phrase, but not the central meaning, of Clifford Geertz, he has described Japan as a 'theater state' (*gekijō kokka*), by which he meant that the nation had always functioned in accordance with someone else's script—first China's, then the West's—rather than its own; that people, especially élites, had always acted out roles of someone else's authorship.[2]

I myself have borrowed a diagram from James White, an American political scientist, to illustrate schematically the lines of inquiry that were set in motion in Japan when the initial equivalence of modernization and westernization and opposition

	Non-Western	Western
Traditional	1	2
Modern	3	4

Fig. 2. Japanese discourse about modernization

of tradition and modernity came into question (see Fig. 2). As White put it, when one assumes that what is modern is also Western, and vice versa, the resultant mental image is of a two-by-two matrix with two empty cells; everything that exists in non-Western societies can then be located either in cell 1 (non-Western, non-modern) or cell 4 (Western, modern).[3] This indeed was the mainstream view in the early Meiji period, and to a great extent it reflected reality: most of what was modern in Japan then, primarily objects, was Western, not only by invention but also by manufacture. Discourse about modernization at the time was structured along a diagonal axis between cells 1 and 4, the one containing 'evil practices of the past' and the other, all that modernizing élites considered useful, just, and good. Thereafter, however, a shift in the direction of discourse occurred: concern focused increasingly on the vertical relationship between cells 1 and 3 and the horizontal relationship between cells 3 and 4. In both cases, cell 3—the locus, real or desired, of what was both modern *and* Japanese—came into prominence. I will have more to say about the contents of cell 3 later, but now I want to turn to the first of the three periods I have identified.

The 1880s and 1890s

There had, of course, been disagreements over modernization prior to the 1880s, but I think the debate that began in that decade was qualitatively different from what went on before. In the first place, it was carried on by members of a self-conscious 'new generation', who felt they spoke as and on behalf of the 'youth of

Meiji'. They rejected as outmoded or misguided the ideas of those they called 'the old men of Tempō'—that is, the leaders of the government and such people as Fukuzawa Yukichi, one of the early champions of modernization, who had been born in the Tempō era (1830–44). Born themselves in the 1850s and 1860s, the new generation had experienced the new educational system that the old men of Tempō had merely designed or encouraged. And they had reached its highest extant levels, where, under the guidance primarily of foreign teachers, they studied the works of Macaulay, Tocqueville, Spencer, Mill, Rousseau, Buckle, Carlyle, and Hegel. As a group of them announced on one occasion: 'It is easier for us to read the novels of [Walter] Scott than to read the *Genji Monogatari*',[4] a novel written by Murasaki Shikibu, lady-in-waiting to the empress, in the early eleventh century.

Secondly, unlike members of the older generation who had disagreed and sometimes fought over specific policies and, occasionally, over the very advisability of any change at all, the concerns of the new generation were more general. They concurred on the advisability of modernization; their debate centered on what kind of modernization Japan needed.

On the one hand were those who equated modernization with westernization and urged much more of it. As Tokutomi Sohō, a leading spokesman for this view, put it: 'We have imported Western techniques, politics, scholarship, etc, and we hope now to build a Western society. Therefore we must also import the Western code of ethics, which alone can coexist with the progress of knowledge.'[5] Or Kozaki Hiromichi: 'We must rid ourselves of Oriental traits.... We must not ... simply adopt the externals of Western customs; we must go further and reform people's minds as well'.[6]

On the other hand there were those groping for a different definition of modernization. They were not, I should emphasize, interested in promoting 'Western techniques and Eastern morality'. That was an old formula their generation had rejected. Rather, they sought a Japanese path to modernity that did not necessarily preclude Western values.

As Shiga Shigetaka wrote: 'I enthusiastically urge the importation of Western ways, but I cannot agree with the argument that there is nothing of beauty, no special talent, nothing refined in Japanese civilization and that we must therefore imitate Western styles, uproot the whole of Western civilization and transplant it in Japanese soil.'[7] Or Kuga Katsunan:

> Differences in wealth and ability among individuals are unavoidable; but despite these differences, no individual should scorn and demean himself. [We believe] that a nation, just as an individual, must have a feeling of pride in order to exist. There are differences in wealth and power among all countries. Compared to European countries Japan is weak, but . . . she ought not to be frightened into self-abasement. . . . National independence . . . always requires national pride.[8]

What surfaced here, in an outpouring of magazine and newspaper articles as well as books, were conflicting views of both Japanese and world history. The advocates of modernization-as-westernization belittled, indeed rejected, all of Japan's past, both recent and remote. Their critics were uncomfortable with finding Scott easier to read than Lady Murasaki. Aware that the West was not an undifferentiated whole and that the peoples of Western countries fiercely defended their separate identities, they thought Japan must do the same. The nation, in their view, could not exist on borrowed culture; it needed a cultural identity of its own to survive and flourish, and that in turn required a re-evaluation of Japan's past.

But contrasting views of world history (and the world's future) were involved as well. It is interesting to note that each side drew much of its ammunition from the works of Herbert Spencer, although from different emphases within his writings. Tokutomi and other 'westernizers' argued that the evolution of societies from a militant to an industrial phase, as set forth in Spencer's *Principles of Sociology*, was indeed universal. Timing might differ, but every society followed the same, unilinear course, or it disappeared. Britain, France, and the United States were furthest along that course, revealing the future Japan must pursue.

Miyake Setsurei, another member of the group seeking a Japanese path to modernity, preferred to draw upon the social Darwinism in Spencer's thought. Positing the existence of 'world civilization' as the functional equivalent of a species, he argued that it could develop fully only if nations, the present units of competition, exercised their interests and contributed their special talents. So far Western nations had made the greatest contributions, but it was essential for other cultures to play their part if world civilization was to progress to an even higher stage. It followed that Japan had an obligation, not merely to itself but to the world as well, to preserve and develop its unique qualities.

By the mid-1890s the debate among members of the 'new generation' had ended in a qualified victory for the advocates of a Japanese path to modernity. What had turned the tide against the advocates of thoroughgoing westernization was less the power of their opponents' arguments than disillusionment with the West and with Spencerian views of development. In the early 1890s, for example, Tokutomi began writing about the 'civilization sickness' (*bunmei byō*) that corrupted simple, rugged virtues and produced weakness, and about the need for a 'union of barbaric vigor and civilized learning'.[9] Spencer's industrial phase was not bringing peace and prosperity, an end to all the armed conflict of the preceding militant phase. Therefore Japan had better concentrate on developing and preserving the rugged qualities that Westerners were losing. Like Shiga, Kuga, and Miyake, he had begun looking to Japan's past—in his case, to the country's 'rugged' martial traditions—for the elements of a cultural identity and a secure future. Unlike them, however, he focused on Japan's destiny alone. Absent from his thought, and from most of the influential writing about modernization at the turn of the century, was a broader concern with the development of world civilization. It was Japan, and Japan alone, that mattered.

The 1920s and 1930s

Historical interpretations of Japan in the 1920s and 1930s are in a state of flux. An older paradigm, crystallized in the early 1960s, has come under fire in the past fifteen years or so, both in Japan and in the West. As yet no rival paradigm has gained full acceptance; instead, new lines of inquiry have been pursued, and a number of studies that implicitly or explicitly challenge the received view have been published.

The older—perhaps I should say the existing—paradigm emphasizes the contrasts between the two decades, and by extension finds links between the 1920s and the postwar era. The 1920s were a time of liberalism, internationalism, and, hence, of 'healthy' modernization. By contrast, the 1930s was a fascist, or a militarist, era; it was characterized by a failure of freedom, retrogression in foreign policy decision-making, a breakdown in modernization. Only after the catharsis of defeat in war and the reforms of the Occupation, which built upon the stymied progress of the 1920s, did Japan get back 'on course'.

Critics of this paradigm, of whom I am one, tend to stress the continuities between the 1920s and the 1930s, and by extension the links between the 1930s and the postwar era. In much of this revisionist writing there is a tendency to see the war not as an aberration in Japan's development but as an outcome of that development. This does not amount to an attempt to justify the war, but is an effort to explain it in terms of evolutionary change, rather than of retrogression or breakdown.

Quite obviously, these differing perspectives influence analyses of Japanese discourse about modernization during the decades in question. According to the older paradigm, that discourse was a lopsided affair between a few cosmopolitan individuals on the one hand and the military and its ultra-nationalistic sympathizers on the other; between advocates of pursuing a westernizing future (cell 4) and advocates of a wholesale and disastrous embrace of nativism that was anti-West and therefore anti-modern (cell 1). The latter silenced the former by means of arrest or other, more subtle forms of intimidation.

I think this view distorts the historical realities of the period, as well as distorting, or oversimplifying, the thought of some of the individuals cited in discussions of it. More importantly, it focuses on what were, in my opinion, the fringes of discourse at the time, ignoring the mainstream; on extreme, and sometimes eccentric, opinion rather than on the more ordinary and representative. What I have to say about these two decades relates to the latter.

Among some of the most capable and respected scholars, journalists, novelists, bureaucrats, and Diet members, one finds virtually no advocacy of nativism.

It is sometimes said that nativism was rife among poets and novelists of the time, especially the romantics; that, like scholars of national studies (*kokugaku*) in the late Tokugawa period who rejected Chinese influences on Japan, many sought a return to an unalloyed culture of an earlier time in order to achieve spiritual wholeness. Yet closer inspection of what they wrote indicates that they knew this was impossible, knew that the past was irretrievably out of reach. As Tanizaki Jun'ichirō observed in *In Praise of Shadows*, a long essay published in 1934, the bright lights of Western culture had exacted a heavy toll on the traditional Japanese arts that thrive in semi-darkness. He lamented the crassness of the fountain pen, the harshness of Western paper, the garishness of gas heaters, and he went on to observe 'how unlucky we have been in comparison with the Westerner [who] has been able to move forward in ordered steps, while we have met superior civilization and have had to surrender to it . . . to leave a road we have followed for thousands of years'. Perhaps if Japan had been left alone, the Japanese might 'one day have discovered our own substitute for the trolley, the radio, the airplane of today. They would have been no borrowed gadgets, they would have been tools of our own culture, suited to us.' But he also knew that he was dreaming, 'that having come this far we cannot turn back'. His hope was that in literature something of the 'world of shadows' could perhaps be preserved; 'in the mansion called literature', if nowhere else, he 'would have the eaves deep and the walls dark'.[10]

Like contemporary novelists and poets, other Japanese intellectuals were concerned in the 1930s about the corrosive effects of Western culture, but it was not electricity and other mundane facets of life that bothered them. Instead, their criticism focused on Western modalities of political, social, and economic organization: on parliamentary process, individualism, free enterprise. Like Tanizaki, they knew there was no turning back. The answer lay in moving forward, but in a direction different from before:

Japan needed to break away not from modernity but from modernity defined and exemplified by the West. By the late 1930s they had persuaded themselves that their goal should be a new cultural order at home and in East Asia.

What is most significant about the intellectuals who championed this 'new order' in the 1930s is that many of them had been champions of liberalism and/or Marxism a decade earlier. The basic trend of the interwar decades, then, was not the displacement of one group of thinkers by another, but rather a shift in the thinking of the same men.

The philosopher Miki Kiyoshi (1895–1945) provides an example of this evolutionary process. Like others of his generation, he had been disturbed by the tangible evidence of class conflict in Japan in the 1910s and early 1920s, and he had felt that reforms were needed to accommodate working-class grievances. At the start of his career he had believed that Marxism provided the necessary diagnosis of the situation and the means of resolving it. By the late 1920s, however, his views were beginning to change. In a series of articles he portrayed Marxism as an ideological response to the rise of the proletariat in the nineteenth century, that is, as a time-bound philosophy rather than a universal truth. Subsequently, in the early 1930s, he concluded that both liberalism and Marxism had become obsolete. The problems facing Japan were the same as previously, but now a new solution, reflecting the realities of the twentieth century, was required. As he saw it, the solution lay in the state as an agent of reform, because only the state could transcend the narrow interests of individuals or groups.

At the same time he was critical of those who asserted that Japan could solve its problems by a vague 'return to tradition'. What was necessary was an understanding of Japanese tradition, not some mythical, imagined view of the past. In his assessment, the distinguishing characteristic of Japanese culture was its eclecticism and flexibility. This had been demonstrated in the past; now it was time to demonstrate it again, by breaking away from the present impasse in which Japan found itself and making a real contribution to world civilization. Japan could do this, he thought, by means of 'cooperativism', the harnessing of the spirit of close ties of kinship found in rural communities, in which the individual placed the welfare of the whole above his own selfish interests, to the scientific spirit of the West. The result would be a uniquely Asian spirit, untainted by the evils of capitalism or the insidious doctrine of individualism. It would, in his view, enable Japan not only to solve its own problems, but also to win the support of Chinese nationalists, liberate China from Western imperialism, and hence permit the Orient to determine its own destiny.

Miki accepted an offer to join the Showa Research Association in the late 1930s, became director of its Cultural Problems Research Group, and as such became an architect of Japan's plans for a self-sufficient co-prosperity sphere in Asia. He, like most other intellectuals, regarded the war that resulted as an act of creation—an attempt to realize a new conception of society—not as an act of desperation or destruction. In terms of Professor Yano's metaphor, Japan was at last ceasing to be a 'theater state' and was attempting to write its own script. To be sure, this euphoria did not last for long, and an awareness of the havoc their country had wrought was to make many of the intellectuals who had embraced the Pan-Asianism of the late 1930s, and who, unlike Miki, survived Japan's defeat and occupation, wary of Japanese definitions of modernity for a long time to come.

The 1970s and 1980s

I now arrive at the last of the three periods under review, the 1970s and 1980s, and what is known as *Nihonjinron*, or the debate about Japaneseness. A trickle of scholarly articles in the 1960s about the origins of the Japanese people and the Japanese language suddenly surged, in the early 1970s, into a flood of books and essays on a wide range of topics related to Japanese culture and Japan's role in the contemporary world. Aimed at a mass audience, these writings, and a simultaneous flood of television programs in a similar vein, both reflected and helped to intensify a shift in popular attitudes toward Japan's past and, by extension, toward its present and future course.

I do not share the alarm expressed by some Westerners when confronted with this literature. True, some of it—for example, an exploration of the difference between Japanese and Western excrement—strikes me as rather far-fetched and silly. Nor am I persuaded, as Tsunoda Tadanobu would have me be,[11] that the brains of the Japanese differ from those of all other peoples in the world. But these I regard as extreme examples in a fundamentally serious effort on the part of the Japanese to recapture a sense of their own history and formulate their own cultural identity.

During the Occupation and on through the next fifteen years or so, Japan's past values and institutions were widely denigrated by the Japanese, as had been the case in the early Meiji years of commitment to Western-style 'civilization and enlightenment'. As Kenneth Pyle has observed:

Dominant opinion held that prewar nationalism, which had been built on extraordinary claims of the collectivist ethic, the Japanese family-state, and the emperor system, had led them astray. Particularism had blinded them to their real self-interest, had overcome their best instincts, and had reduced them to international outcasts. How better to redeem themselves in the eyes of the world than by turning their backs on the particular claims of nationality and proclaiming themselves citizens of the world! Therefore, not only did they embrace [the] liberal values and institutions [established by the Occupation]; they were enthusiastically swept up into the mystique of a noble experiment.... To the extent that Japanese institutions and values diverged from the Western pattern, they were seen as somehow abnormal, distorted, unhealthy, and pre-modern. If Japan was to recover and develop into a modern, democratic and progressive industrial society, it must eliminate these values and institutions, and follow the path of the liberal-democratic nations of the West.[12]

In short, the Japanese—with a powerful boost from the Occupation authorities—had once again focused their attention on cells 1 and 4 of Figure 2, observed earlier. Modernization was once again equated with westernization, modernity once again viewed as the opposite of tradition. With the passage of time, however, and with the growing recognition at home and abroad of Japan's economic achievements, this proved increasingly unsatisfactory. As had occurred twice previously, the discourse

Modernization and its Discontents

about modernization intensified, and attention once more focused on the search for what was both modern *and* Japanese.

Amid the considerable diversity of the resultant flood of books and essays, one can, I think, identify two major and related themes. The first is doubt about the continued validity of the West as a model for Japan. Europe may be a fine venue for sightseeing, wrote one scholar, but it no longer has anything to teach Japan. England had fallen victim to the 'British Disease' (*Eikoku byō*), asserted others, defining the malady as 'a social disease which, upon the advancement of welfare programs, causes a diminished will to work, over-emphasis on rights, and declining productivity'. An 'American Disease' was also identified: 'a wasteful, inefficient society, bereft of its work ethic, no longer able to maintain the quality of its goods, crime- and divorce-ridden, suffering social disintegration'. 'Watching the United States suddenly losing its magnificence', an editorial writer for a major newspaper observed in 1980, 'is like watching a former lover's beauty wither away'.[13]

The second theme is the direct bearing of Japanese cultural traditions on Japan's contemporary achievements. One of the more interesting, and widespread, arguments in this vein concerns the collectivist ethic. Reviled in the early postwar period as a pillar of prewar nationalism, it was increasingly seen in the 1970s and 1980s as a positive force in national life. As an economic study group appointed by the prime minister to advise on the future management of the economy reported in 1980:

Unlike Western societies [which are based] on the 'individual' or 'self', the basic characteristic of Japanese culture is that, as shown in the Japanese word *ningen* [human being], it values the 'relationship between persons' (*hito to hito no aidagara*). In examining Japanese culture closely, we discover that this basic characteristic permeates, and acts as a living foundation of, the workings and the system of the Japanese economy. Rather than encouraging intense competition among individuals, with each being wholly responsible for his actions, the Japanese economy relies on 'collegial groups' (*nakama shūdan*) that are based on various relationships created within and between companies. This tends to give rise to a phenomenon of dependence (*amae*) that is induced by mutual reliance (*motareai*) among persons. In some instances, such a relationship can be detrimental to 'freedom' and 'competition'.... However, the Japanese economy... [as exemplified in the word] *ningen*, is the very model which Western societies are now beginning to emulate.[14]

Implicit in this statement, and many others like it, is a rejection of the so-called convergence hypothesis, which states that there is a universal logic to industrialism and that the social relationships found in the first nations to industrialize (individualism, a free labor market, and so on) must inevitably develop elsewhere. The statement tells us that the Japanese economy has developed to where it is, and will continue developing, not in spite of 'collegiality' but because of it. It also implies that there are multiple paths to modernity. To return to Figure 2, it is asserting that, just as movement occurred from cell 2 to cell 4 in the West, so too there has been movement from cell 1 to cell 3 in Japan—from the non-modern and non-Western to the modern and non-Western. Indeed, it goes on to suggest that there is now the possibility, in fact the desirability, of movement from cell 4 to cell 3—from the modern and Western to the modern and Japanese.

Whether or not one agrees with these implicit assertions, they should be seen as representing a qualitative change from efforts to fill cell 3 earlier in the postwar era, and hence they help us map a shift in the locus of Japanese pride. In the 1960s the Japanese could point only to objects such as the electric rice cooker or freeze-dried noodles as their very own contributions to modernity; in the 1970s and 1980s, they began pointing to values and institutions (most notably, employment practices and strategies for managing production) that have been shaped by their own historical experience. Their doing so is in some respects reminiscent of earlier attempts by the new generation of the Meiji era and by men such as Miki Kiyoshi in the 1930s, but I think it is important to keep the differences as well as the similarities in mind. Earlier discourse about modernization was marked by a sense of anguish or of impasse that one finds little, if any, evidence of more recently; it was a product of the recognition that in certain key respects Japan was less powerful than the nations of the West. During the 1970s and 1980s discourse was marked by a sense of achievement and flowed from the recognition that Japan was one of the most fully modern nations in the world. What formerly centered on the identification of problems to be solved had to a notable extent become the celebration of goals attained.

Critics of *Nihonjinron* tend to ignore these differences and to see in the similarities with the 1890s and 1930s signs of a disturbing resurgence of nativism. Japan, in their view, is once again in danger of veering 'off course'. As indicated previously, I do not subscribe to this view, or to its underlying assumption that only one correct form of modernity—that achieved by the West—exists. What the similarities with the past suggest to me is that in *Nihonjinron* we are confronted with the latest manifestation of one of the central issues in modern Japanese thought: how to reconcile foreign borrowing with cultural identity.

Unwilling to take the easier path and claim that they actually invented many of the objects and ideas that the contemporary West was putting to use—as have, for example, the Hindu nationalists who claimed that India invented the airplane centuries ago—the Japanese have been forced during the past one hundred years or so to grapple with the implications of dependence on external stimuli for much of what they valued. They have derived only temporary comfort from the belief that Western experience revealed universal truths and universally valid patterns of development. The crunch has always come when the ultimate outcome of accepting that belief—the demise of Japanese culture and identity—was seriously considered. And they have always (although *not* always in the same mood or mode) looked back to their own history and into their own traditions to regain a sense of themselves.

On the whole, this has been a creative rather than a scholarly undertaking, in that it has been based primarily on an idealized and imagined, not a closely studied and well-documented, past. This makes it relatively easy to poke holes in many of the assertions made about Japan's uniqueness (as, indeed, one can do for the claims to uniqueness made by the citizens of most other nations), but to do so without consideration of the underlying reasons why those assertions have been and continue to be made is to impede, not promote, understanding of the phenomenon.

7 | The Postwar 'Economic Miracle' and its Consequences

When Japan surrendered to the Allies in August 1945, its economy lay in ruins. A significant share of the nation's industrial plant and housing stock, and almost all of its merchant marine, had been destroyed. Supplies of imported fuel and raw materials were depleted, and no trade permitted. Agricultural production languished at about 60 per cent of its level in 1941, leaving many urban residents desperately short of food. Runaway inflation threatened. It took fully a decade for recovery to the levels of economic output prevailing on the eve of the Second World War to be achieved. Then what is often described as the 'economic miracle' began. Instead of slackening to the lower levels prevailing in most other industrialized countries, growth rates in Japan continued at an average annual rate of some 10 per cent until the early 1970s.

By 1968 Japan had surpassed West Germany in overall gross national product, to rank as the third largest economy in the world, outdistanced only by the (then) Soviet Union and the United States. Not surprisingly, this dramatic development in the nation's fortunes, and the continued—albeit slower—growth of the Japanese economy during the 1970s and 1980s, generated considerable interest elsewhere in the world. Indeed, it is fair to say that of all the books and articles published about Japan in the West during the past twenty years or so, those probing for the 'secrets' of Japan's postwar economic success are far and away the most numerous.

What has emerged from the best of this literature—by which I mean those studies that are based on solid empirical research—is an explication of some complexity and dynamism. As is usually the case, a variety of causal factors can be identified, and the importance of any one among them has shifted over time. There is also a 'downside' to the story. As economists of all persuasions are wont to tell us, there is no such thing as a free lunch, and by the early 1970s the Japanese people had become acutely aware that high rates of economic growth were far from an unmixed blessing. Let us begin with the 'miracle' of rapid growth and then turn to consider its social costs.

The 'Economic Miracle'

In a tongue-in-cheek essay that appeared on the opinion page of the *New York Times* on 4 March 1981, the diplomatic historian John Curtis Perry urged the Japanese to 'Return the Favor: Occupy Us'. Noting that '[a]fter World War II Americans spent 80 months in Japan building a peace-loving, democratic, and self-supporting society', he observed that it was now time for Japan to reciprocate: 'Without a preliminary war, we should ask the Japanese to come here . . . and do exactly those things we did for them from 1945 to 1952.' By 'those things' he meant: (1) amending the American constitution to renounce war, so that 'vast Federal revenues hitherto going to the defense budget would be freed for loans to rejuvenate and rebuild decaying industrial plant'; (2) reforming the tax system without any 'interference by special-interest groups' and 'making a balanced budget immediate reality rather than pious rhetoric'; (3) providing substantial financial aid to assist in the rebuilding of the economy, while enforcing austerity to insure that aid was not squandered on immediate improvements in living standards; and (4) strengthening democracy by rooting out monopolistic or oligopolistic practices in business and agriculture, forcing almost all high-ranking decision-makers in government and industry into retirement to make way for fresh young leadership and insisting that a clause granting women the same legal rights as men be included in the new Japanese-inspired constitution. 'The American people would cheerfully cooperate with the occupiers', Perry continued,

> because the sincerity of the Japanese, their friendliness, their obvious good intentions, would smooth over the inevitable blunders and misunderstandings caused by their ignorance of American customs. Any American resentment would be directed instead toward our own leaders who had got us into the mess in the first place, not at the Japanese who were so obviously trying to help us get out of it.

Here, in inverted and satiric form, is a particularly succinct rendering of what then was and probably still is a widespread view in the United States: that the reforms carried out during the Occupation, and the aid provided by a generous America (including provision of an enduring 'nuclear umbrella' under which Japan could shelter), had led directly to Japan's 'economic miracle'. It was a 'favor' for which the Japanese should be eternally grateful.

The tenacity with which many Americans have held to this view over the years does not, of course, make it true. In fact, the more closely one examines the causes of sustained high rates of economic growth in Japan during the 1950s and 1960s, the less central the Occupation era becomes. For reasons far more closely related to the emerging cold war in the late 1940s than to generosity of spirit toward a humbled adversary, the Americans did abandon their original plan to transfer much of Japan's remaining capacity in heavy industry to the neighboring states in Asia which the Japanese war machine had ravaged and began instead to focus attention on making Japan an economically and politically viable ally in the region. This shift in aims, and more particularly the American's use of Japan as their main logistical base after the outbreak of the Korean War in 1950, gave a much-needed boost to the Japanese economy. Also important in sustaining the benefits of that boost was the willingness of the United States in the early 1950s to sponsor Japan's re-entry into the international trading system, from which it had been excluded—first by its own belligerent actions and then by the terms of its surrender and occupation—since 1941. These and other American initiatives were certainly important in enabling the Japanese to rebuild their economy to the levels of output prevailing in the mid- to late 1930s—that is, in the process of economic *recovery* from the war. The so-called miracle, however, still lay ahead, in the continuation of high rates of growth *after* recovery had been achieved. It was this later growth which enabled Japan to lunge forward from the ranks of minor industrial countries to the status of 'economic superpower', and this was substantially a Japanese achievement.

The first and arguably most crucial step the Japanese took was to toss aside the model of their economic future bequeathed to them by the Occupation. Surveying the economy for which they were temporarily responsible, Occupation economists had decided that Japan should exploit its one great advantage, a plentiful supply of labor, to become the 'workshop of Asia', producing such relatively low value-added items as textiles, pottery, and toys for sale in the international market-place. High-technology goods would be imported from the advanced nations of the West (chief among them, the United States), which were favorably endowed with the natural resources such as iron ore, crude oil, and aluminum essential to their production. This model came close to replicating what the Japanese had achieved by the late 1920s and, according to one estimate,[1] had Japan remained content with it, its level of per capita disposable income in the early 1970s would have been on a par with the levels prevailing in some of the more prosperous nations of Latin America. That it had achieved Italian levels of per capita income instead, and was poised to forge ahead of France and the United Kingdom was owing to the decision, taken by government officials but warmly supported by business leaders and the general public, to return to what had been Japan's goal since early in the Meiji era: to become a 'first-class' country with a fully industrialized, state-of-the-art economy.

As early as 1946, relatively low-ranking bureaucrats had drafted a series of recommendations for the reconstruction of the Japanese economy which stressed the importance of continuing the prewar trend of the movement of labor from agriculture to industry and the further modernization of the industrial sector. Circumstances then and for some years hence dictated an initial emphasis on light, labor-intensive industries, as in the Occupation model, but the foreign exchange earned from exports of what eventually came to be dismissed as 'Asian manufactures' was to be used to acquire the advanced technology of the West and for the promotion of heavy, capital-intensive industry. With the publication of its New Long-Range Economic Plan in December of 1957, the Japanese government made it clear that the static and somewhat self-serving model devised by the Occupation had been replaced by a dynamic development plan that would, if successful, bridge the economic gap between Japan and the leading nations of the world.

Plans in themselves do not make economic miracles—not even in early postwar Japan, where key ministries of state enjoyed a high degree of control over access to the foreign exchange that all would-be heavy industrialists in the private sector needed. Had the international economic environment been less favorable to the strategy officials put forward, or had Japanese capitalists, managers, and workers been less enthusiastic about it, things might well have turned out differently.

As we saw in Chapter 3, Japan's early industrialization was facilitated by a generally favorable climate of economic expansion elsewhere in the world and by commitment to ideas of free trade in the technologically more advanced West. This was also the case in the 1950s and 1960s. Indeed, Japan's continued economic transformation as set forth in government plans during the postwar period was predicated on the existence of similarly favorable conditions, principally the availability of industrial raw materials and fuel at low prices, general growth in world GNP, and expanding world trade. When the first of those conditions came to a sudden end in 1973, with the 'oil crisis' induced by the Organization of Petroleum Exporting Countries (OPEC), so too did the Japanese 'economic miracle', for Japan's growth to that point had been highly dependent on movement into such energy-intensive industries as steel and petrochemicals, and 99.7 per cent of the oil consumed in Japan was imported. Nevertheless, the window of opportunity had lasted long enough to yield results and reserves of wealth that could be put to other economic uses.

It is more difficult to assess the economic impact of what has become known as 'Japan's free ride on defense' during this same period. The facts are that the United States provided for Japan's basic national security throughout the cold war era and that no more than 1 per cent of Japan's GNP was spent on maintaining the ground, air, and maritime self-defense forces Japan itself established in the early 1950s. That Japan's neighbors—or, for that matter, the United States—would have tolerated greater Japanese spending on defense during these years is highly unlikely, but no such attempt was made. Instead Japan maintained a 'low', deferential posture in regional and international affairs and concentrated its resources on economic development. Had the legacy of the war been more easily transcended and had the United States been less determined to dominate the free world's campaign against communism in Asia, Japan might have come to shoulder increased international responsibilities, and some of what the country had been investing in growth would then have been spent on arms. According to one attempt to quantify the economic impact of this highly counterfactual scenario,[2] had Japan spent 6 to 7 per cent of its GNP on defense during the 1950s and 1960s (at a time when the United States was spending about 8 per cent), and had resources which might otherwise have gone into investment in the economy been used for this purpose, with no beneficial 'spillovers' from military to civilian uses of technology to mitigate the loss, Japan's growth rate would have declined from 10 to 8 per cent per year. As a result, its GNP in the early 1970s would have been one-third smaller than it was in actuality: in other words, a less dramatic 'economic miracle' than West Germany's, but one which still would have placed Japan firmly among the leading industrial nations of the world.

If we shift our attention back from the counterfactual to the real, we come to the decisive factors. In theory, and to a great extent in practice, all fully or partially industrialized countries—even some 'under-developed' countries—were in a position to benefit from the favorable international economic climate of the postwar era. That Japan benefited at a more rapid rate was owing to actions taken and emotions kindled within Japan itself.

The latter, although resistant to quantification and hence vexing to economists, were of considerable importance. While a small number of officials turned their attention in the mid-1940s to grappling with Japan's longer range economic future, many Japanese grappled with survival from day to day. What little they eventually accumulated over and above their subsistence needs they used to begin replacing the possessions they had lost, or pawned, during the final years of the war or the early hard years of occupation. Like those who had survived the same war elsewhere, they had seen an ordinary, fairly predictable world shattered and had learned to take nothing for granted. That their own country was held responsible for the conflict in Asia added to their disillusionment.

From this came, with some official encouragement, a widespread commitment to redemption for themselves and for the nation through hard work in the cause of economic growth. The Japanese could no longer rejoice in their empire, and the once-celebrated exploits of their army and navy were now denigrated as the source of their ruination, but each notch upward in GNP or in international market share for ships or transistor radios could and did give a boost to national pride. By the mid-1950s, when recovery had been attained and when all subsequent growth represented new achievement, what some observers have termed a 'GNP nationalism' became manifest. That every Japanese reveled in the daily economic news on radio or television with an intensity akin to that of the dedicated football or baseball fan in the West, as some accounts would have us believe, is unlikely, but without doubt a growth-oriented psychology prevailed. The psychology of insecurity that underlay it, even after the worst years of hardship had passed, gave the country's political and economic leaders considerable freedom of action in taking steps to promote further economic growth.

The main contribution of the state was in the creation and maintenance over an extended period of policies favorable to growth. Those reforms of the Occupation era that reflected the

American notion that business must be regulated to curb the excesses to which it was prone were quietly ignored, and emphasis was placed on promoting an environment in which business could flourish, technological improvements escalate, and exports increase. This emphasis resulted, among other things, in tax codes that favored income from savings and capital gains over income from wages and in the concentration of state spending on such social overheads as railways, roads, and electrical power that were of direct benefit to industry and commerce.

The impact of these macroeconomic policies was intensified by the state's industrial policy, which evolved from fairly modest beginnings in the immediate aftermath of the war into an effective system of industrial targeting by the mid-1950s. Targeted industries were of two kinds, those thought to have a promising future at home and in export markets and those thought to be facing declining demand and/or increasing foreign competition. Declining (or sunset) industries were eligible for guidance on diversification into other economic activities and on the retraining of their workers; temporary mergers of competing firms might be encouraged, to allow the remaining economies of scale to be wrested from production. Promising (or sunrise) industries were granted access to low-cost loans and, in some instances, to direct subsidies; a variety of tax and depreciation incentives to encourage investment and reward increases in the share of exports in their total sales; the duty-free import of essential machinery and equipment; and protection from foreign competition by means of tariff and non-tariff barriers. Although political considerations did at times interfere with the pure economic rationality of this system, its basic premise was honored over time: assistance which cost the state money was reserved for new industries that would propel the Japanese economy forward.

There are two other features of the system that are worthy of note as well. The first is that its champions—chiefly but not exclusively officials of the Ministry of International Trade and Industry (MITI)—regarded targeting as an ongoing process, not a once-and-for-all setting of direction for the economy. Just as Japan was moving into realms previously dominated by the more advanced economies of the West, so too would other, currently weak, economies move into realms now dominated by Japan. This dynamic view of economic development, engendered in large part by Japan's own history, made constant study of both the developing and developed world essential and necessitated recurrent targeting, far in advance of the loss of comparative advantage to an emerging rival or of a new opportunity to an established one, to secure the desired outcomes for Japan.

The second point is that Japanese industry did not sit on its hands waiting for MITI or some other government ministry to tell it which way to jump. On the contrary, the initiative for many new economic departures in the early postwar years came from industrialists and entrepreneurs, and only when promising results had been achieved did bureaucrats step in to facilitate the success of these ventures by making available the foreign exchange or export credits they required. Just as the founders of the Sony Corporation had to lobby a skeptical MITI for permission to import transistors for the radios they hoped to produce, so too did Japanese steelmakers have to overcome MITI's conviction in the early 1950s that there was no way for Japan to challenge American ascendancy in that sphere by effecting significant improvements in productivity on their own. While these may well be extreme examples, they remind us that Japan's was a private enterprise economy, in which most of the important economic decisions were made within each enterprise, or within the trade associations and enterprise groups (*kigyō shūdan*) that soon emerged to assist participating firms in long-term forecasting, expanding their respective market shares, and—not unimportantly—devising strategies to maximize the benefits to them of government policies while minimizing bureaucratic interference in their operations. At no point did the bureaucracy possess legal powers to enforce its targeting strategies. As noted previously, its leverage was enhanced in the early postwar years by tight state controls over access to foreign exchange and other scarce resources, but as recovery and growth progressed these resources became ever more widely available, and increasingly the bureaucracy had to rely on persuasion, frequent consultation with a wide range of business interests, and an accumulating record of basically sound advice to secure compliance.

Underlying the success of 'administrative guidance', the term by which this particular form of bureaucratic influence over the economy came to be known, and more generally of the pro-business macroeconomic policies of the government, was the energetic behavior of the Japanese business community. The forced retirement of leading capitalists and industrialists tainted with complicity in Japan's war effort (to which Perry referred in his *New York Times* essay) thrust a somewhat younger generation of mid-level managerial personnel into positions of authority within many established enterprises. Whether their older and, as it happened, only temporarily disgraced superiors would have reacted to dire economic necessity with the same zeal cannot be known for certain, but the fact remains that most of these newly empowered executive managers demonstrated a considerable enthusiasm for adapting production to peacetime purposes and for reinvesting any profits that were achieved in new technology or expansion. Others with no previous experience in private enterprise, such as recently demobilized soldiers and sailors who possessed a degree of technical knowledge, turned their attention to finding a niche for themselves amid the general confusion of Japan's postwar economic situation. Out of the scramble for survival came an entrepreneurial surge on a scale not seen in Japan since the Meiji era. Production was what mattered, and the seizing of any perceived opportunity to increase it or direct it into new channels was, for the time being, virtually an end in itself. As innovation and the willingness to maintain high rates of reinvestment in promising ventures began to pay off in expanding output and increased sales, an ethos of expansion became institutionalized. Growth itself conferred honor on those who achieved it, and the honor induced further attention to growth.

One realm in which corporate managers expended considerable effort during the early postwar years was labor relations and the honing of what subsequently became widely known—but not always accurately portrayed—as the Japanese employment system. Although far less widespread than many accounts would have us believe, and far less a natural expression of the culture than a resolution of long-standing tensions between capital and labor in large-scale modern industry, this system did play an important role in the achievement of high rates of economic growth during the latter part of the 'miracle' era.

As we saw in Chapter 4, workers in heavy industry had begun to organize on a significant scale and to demand improvements in pay and conditions during the 1920s. Thrown on the defensive by a state unwilling to recognize their right to form autonomous unions and engage in collective bargaining, as well as by increasingly unfavorable economic conditions, they had been constrained to curtail their efforts. Although mobilization for war in the mid-1930s had intensified the state's resistance to social conflict within Japan, the war itself had induced the state to take steps to protect the livelihoods of essential workers, most notably by insisting that employers provide them with wages and allowances appropriate to their needs. More generally, officials urged employers to treat workers with respect and to give the factory and workshop discussion councils that had been created at their insistence in many enterprises a meaningful role in the promotion of harmonious labor–management relations. These and other initiatives championed primarily by the Police Bureau of the Home Ministry, the recently established Welfare Ministry, and (somewhat later) the Mobilization Bureau of the Munitions Ministry sought to harness the economy more effectively in the war effort, but to a considerable extent they were predicated on a recognition of the legitimacy of many of the grievances of workers and criticism of prevailing business practice. As the Home Ministry observed in 1941:

Although managers pay lip service to the notion of the enterprise as a family (*jigyō ikka*), in actuality their treatment of workers and staff is fundamentally different. The former are taken care of by labor managers, the latter by personnel managers. The concept governing labor management is that, if the enterprise is a family, the staff are family members and the workers are family servants.[3]

By the end of the war, official exhortation and regulation of employment had begun to put to management on the defensive, and industrial workers were quick to exploit the situation when the Occupation gave them the legal right to do so by means of the Trade Union Law, modeled in part on the American Wagner Act, which went into effect in December 1945. The number of labor unions soared from well-nigh zero at the time of Japan's surrender to more than 17,000 (with almost 5 million members) in 1946 and to almost 34,000 (with over 6.6 million members, some 52 per cent of the total labor force) in 1948. Strike activity swiftly escalated as well, from 920 incidents with 2.7 million participants in 1946 to 1,517 incidents with well over 6 million participants in 1948.

These strikes were not the brief, largely ritualistic 'spring wage offensives' (*shuntō*) for which organized labor in Japan has become known in the West in more recent years, but intense and often protracted battles aimed at achieving guaranteed jobs, wages based on the objective needs of workers (most crucially their age and number of dependents), the elimination of all status distinctions between white-collar staff and blue-collar workers, and a significant voice for workers in the management of enterprises. For almost a decade after 1945 it appeared that this 'social logic of labor', in which enterprises existed primarily to benefit their employees, might win out over the 'economic logic of capital', in which enterprises existed primarily to make money.[4] In the end, however, a counter-offensive launched by management in the late 1940s to regain control over industry in the private sector, sustained throughout the 1950s and early 1960s and subsequently applied to public-sector employment, proved successful.

Citing the threat of communism posed by militant trade unionism, the management of Japan's larger firms increasingly refused to bargain with existing 'first unions', those formed in the immediate aftermath of Japan's surrender—sometimes, but not always, with leadership from among members of the resurgent Japan Communist Party (JCP)—or to renew the agreements made with those unions in the early years after Japan's surrender. More than 10,000 union activists were dismissed from factories and other enterprises in the Red Purge of 1950 and effectively blacklisted from industrial employment in future, on the grounds that they were JCP members who had been plotting revolution. Co-operative 'second unions', which would work with management rather than against it in the interests of the firm and which recognized that management possessed the final say in determining job assignments, work pace, promotions, transfers, and dismissals, were encouraged. Attempts by some labor activists to create effective industry-wide unions that would engage in collective bargaining at the national level were resisted, and the company or enterprise union promoted as the major forum for consultation between management and labor.

This managerial counter-offensive met with considerable resistance from a number of powerful first unions in the electrical power, automobile, steel, coal-mining, and shipbuilding industries during the 1950s and early 1960s, but ultimately the managers of these enterprises, too, prevailed. Like their counterparts in other industries, they did so not only because of the useful backing they received—from the government, the recently established Japan Federation of Employers' Associations (Nikkeiren), and other enterprises (including banks willing to provide loans to enable an embattled firm to withstand a prolonged strike, as happened during a five-month strike at Nissan in 1953)—but also because of their willingness to give in certain areas as they took from their shop-floor employees in others. The long-standing demand of industrial workers for full membership of the enterprise was accepted, and virtually all of the distinctions in dress, on-the-job facilities, and mode of wage or bonus payment between blue- and white-collar workers were eliminated. Rather than rejecting outright the livelihood wages and guaranteed jobs (also known as seniority pay and lifetime employment) which many first unions had secured, managers added an assessment of the 'merit' or 'ability' of the individual worker, as determined by them not by the union, to the former and made it an important element in all personnel decisions, including continued employment. Base pay would be determined by age (and education) at the time of hiring, and annual increases in base pay were assumed to the worker's retirement (at the relatively early age of 55), but the more merit a worker demonstrated on the job, the more likely he would be to receive wages above the base level for his age group and the more likely to be retained or promoted to a higher rank. Merit would be revealed by his loyalty to the firm, his hard work, and his ability to master any new skills the firm required.

The use of the pronouns 'he' and 'his' in the preceding sentences is deliberate, for this settlement applied with very few exceptions to male industrial workers, and to only the minority of them—roughly one-third of all industrial workers in the late 1950s—who worked for firms with more than 300 employees. Women, who made up about 40 per cent of the work force at that time, were almost totally excluded, even if they were employed by larger firms, as were the 'temporary' male employees of those same firms (not a few of them retirees who had worked for the firm in the past and been rehired, without entitlement to any of the benefits they had once enjoyed, at lower rates of pay) and the male employees of the multitude of smaller firms. It was, then, a settlement for the privileged few, not for all Japanese workers, and this is what made it work so effectively in the cause of rapid economic growth.

The settlement enabled the managers of Japan's largest and potentially most profitable firms to transfer workers as they deemed necessary, to dismiss or sidetrack those who did not demonstrate sufficient merit (a defect which for a time included resistance to the idea of a relatively tame second union), and, gradually, to increase the merit element in all workers' pay. By reducing the firm's 'permanent' employees to a minimum and relying on temporary workers or subcontractors during periods of expanding production and sales, managers regained an important degree of control over labor costs. They also gained a method of motivating their core workers to achieve higher productivity, by means of competition among those workers for advancement within the enterprise and of a variety of training and retraining schemes made available to them. Management could therefore afford to invest in the new technology and production processes that were to fuel Japan's rapid growth, with much less concern for the strikes and other forms of opposition by workers in the face of new departures that troubled many corporate managers elsewhere in the world. Those shop-floor workers who had gained full membership of their enterprise were aware that their own futures depended on the future viability of the enterprise itself, and even those with grievances were deterred from undue assertiveness against management by the knowledge that the main alternative employment available to them was in the largely non-unionized sector of small and medium-sized firms, where considerably lower wages, job insecurity, and—at best—a greatly reduced level of such benefits as bonuses, health care, and pensions prevailed. That the number of man-days lost to strikes in Japan declined from an annual average of well over 6 million in the early 1950s to less than 3 million in the late 1960s and, after a brief increase during the early 1970s, to under 1 million by the late 1970s and even less thereafter, is an indication of the success of the management of larger firms in defusing, by compromise as well as by determined resistance, a serious threat to their authority and to the primacy of economic growth in the postwar era.

The Costs of Rapid Economic Growth

During the 1950s and 1960s, high rates of economic growth had been broadly popular within Japan. In addition to the psychological gratification gained from an ever-expanding GNP, there had been more tangible benefits for the people as well. Per capita disposable income had risen from the equivalent of $421 in 1960 to $1,676 in 1970. After scrambling for day-to-day survival in the immediate postwar years, most Japanese households had now managed to acquire the 'three electric treasures': a refrigerator, a washing machine, and a black and white television set. Increasing numbers were in a position to acquire the 'three Cs': color television set, car, and room cooler.[5] Rates of infant mortality were among the very lowest in the world, and rates of longevity were among the very highest. Owing to improved levels of nutrition, boys of 14 years of age were on average 2.5 inches taller than their counterparts in 1940 and girls were 1.25 inches taller (although both suffered from more tooth decay and acne). Their families were increasingly able to afford more schooling for them than the nine years of elementary and middle school made compulsory under the reformed postwar education system.

By the late 1960s, however, there were signs of a shift in public mood. Reports of severe environmental disruption had begun to vie with trade figures and other presumably good economic news in both the print and electronic media, as did reports of Japan's comparatively meager provisions for social security, housing, and leisure. Public attention was beginning to focus on what economists call 'negative externalities' and 'external diseconomies'—that is, on the 'bads' produced along with the 'goods' by modern economic activity—and on the implications of the government's growth-promoting policies.

In 1970 it was reported that the major rivers flowing through the metropolitan areas of Tokyo, Osaka, Fukuoka, and Nagoya were seriously contaminated by human and industrial wastes. High concentrations of eutrophying chemicals were found in the nation's lakes, and so alkaline was the water in a stream running off the seemingly pristine slopes of Mt Fuji that when a journalist dropped a roll of exposed film into it, blurred but recognizable images 'developed'. The proportion of fresh surface water in Japan containing industrial effluents of some kind approximated 100 per cent.

Nor was the damage found limited to fresh surface water. Reports of reduced harvests of ocean products—the source of more than half the annual protein intake of the Japanese people—led the Fisheries Agency of the Ministry of Agriculture, Forestry, and Fisheries to begin monitoring Japan's coastal ocean districts for the presence of mercury and polychlorinated biphenyl (PCB), a chemical widely used in the manufacture of plastics and highly resistant to degradation in the environment. In June of 1973 it announced that PCB counts in excess of the highest permissible density had been detected in a relatively small number of fish caught in nine water-zones within areas covered by eight prefectures; contamination was conspicuous in the Inland Sea. That same month the Ministry of Health and Welfare announced guidelines for the weekly consumption of fish—12 small horse-mackerel, 1.6 yellowfin bass, 47 slices of raw tuna (each weighing 12 grams)—to protect consumers from mercury poisoning. Sales of fish plummeted, much to the consternation of fishermen, fish dealers, and the operators of sushi shops, while consumption of pork skyrocketed.

Contributing powerfully to media and public concern at this time was awareness that heavy metals and PCBs were not merely a potential threat to human life and limb. Two new, pollution-related diseases had already claimed an alarming number of victims. Minamata disease, named after the bay in Kumamoto Prefecture where its occurrence had first been noted some years previously, had been traced to the organic mercury discharged as waste by the Chisso Corporation. Entering the waters of Minamata Bay, the mercury was first absorbed by local fish and then by the bodies of the local residents who consumed the fish. Symptoms of the disease in human beings began with crippling, loss of speech, and sensory motor disturbances, and culminated in coma and death. By 1973, 558 cases had been notified, and 68 deaths reported. *Itai itai* disease (literally, the 'it hurts, it hurts' disease), first reported from Toyama Prefecture, had been traced to the discharge of cadmium by the Mitsui Mining and Smelting Corporation into nearby waters and rice paddies. Some of those who consumed the contaminated rice developed liver and kidney disorders, followed in extreme cases by an agonizing softening of the bones and convulsions of the femoral abductor muscles. By 1972, 123 cases, with 34 deaths, had been reported. The two major staples of the Japanese diet—fish and rice—had been found to be a real threat to human life. The Kanemi rice-bran incident of 1968, when more than 1,000 people in Fukuoka had been poisoned and some 16 killed as a result of eating food cooked with rice-oil into which PCB had been inadvertently mixed during the process of manufacture, intensified concern over the safety of food.

Probably even more alarming, because of the sheer numbers who experienced the problem, was evidence that the air of Japan was far from fit to breathe. Atmospheric pollution in the urban areas of Japan had been recognized as a problem since the late 1950s, but although smoke and soot had been brought under control in the early 1960s, such new, invisible pollutants as sulfur dioxide, nitrogen dioxide, and carbon monoxide had by 1971 reached levels considered dangerous to human health. Tokyo experienced its first severe incidence of poisonous photochemical 'white smog' in 1970, when more than 4,000 cases of skin, eye, and respiratory irritation were reported. During 1971, 24 serious incidents of white smog were recorded in the metropolis, and neighborhood clinics offering relief to local residents, in the form of a brief period at a machine dispensing oxygen, began to appear. According to a survey conducted by the Tokyo Metropolitan Government, some 65 per cent of the city's population believed that they might have to wear gas masks at all times in fifteen years time if nothing were done to tackle the problem. According to the Ministry of Health and Welfare in 1970, more than half of Japan's largest cities experienced atmospheric pollution above the maximum level compatible with human habitation. The number of citizens suffering from such chronic respiratory illnesses as asthma, bronchitis, and emphysema increased; despite the difficulties of establishing medically that such illnesses stemmed from atmospheric pollution, a total of 6,376 cases had been so certified by 1972.

This is a familiar litany of problems, of course, which the resident of any industrialized nation in the 1970s would have recognized. That the situation in Japan appeared especially acute was the result of three related factors. The first was the geographical concentration of industrial activity in Japan (a country only slightly larger in area than Britain) along the Tokaido strip from Tokyo to Kobe, along the northern shore of the Inland Sea, and in northern Kyushu. Although Japan's overall GNP in 1970 was less than one-quarter that of the United States (in land area, some twenty-five times the size of Japan), in terms of GNP per square kilometer it was more than four times as great. In terms of level land—only some 15 per cent of total land surface—where both industry and population have congregated, Japan's GNP was some ten times that of the United States.

The second was the rapid expansion during the 1950s and 1960s of industries making intensive use of natural resources. Energy consumption per square kilometer increased from 293 tons in 1960 to 782 tons in 1969. While energy supplied from coal declined and energy supplied from hydroelectric power remained stable, the use of fuel oil as an energy source increased more than sevenfold to 68 per cent of the total. Along with that increase came a greater volume of hydrocarbon effluents and other forms of pollution from oil. The use of minerals such as lead, aluminum, and zinc known to have a severe environmental impact also increased, as did the use of water for industrial purposes. The share in total water consumption of those industries with serious potential for pollution—most notably, factories producing chemicals and paper pulp—rose from 20 per cent in 1960 to 61.3 per cent in 1968.

The third was the high, virtually unassailable priority given to economic growth throughout the early postwar decades. As discussed earlier, Japan's economy had become a 'growth machine', with increases in output and market share extolled as the nation's salvation from the physical and psychological devastation of defeat in war. In that climate, and the concomitant freedom industries enjoyed from interference by government regulatory agencies, industrialists could and did avoid costly waste-control expenditures. It has been estimated, for example, that in most industrialized countries in the early 1970s some 10 to 20 per cent of the productive facilities in paper-making were devoted to the treatment of poisonous residues. In Japan, pulp mills used most of that 10 to 20 per cent for added production. Similarly, Japanese steelmakers dispensed with the expensive dust-collecting equipment needed on state-of-the-art furnaces and used the money saved (estimated at about 30 per cent of set-up costs) for other more profitable purposes.

Following closely in the wake of growing public concern over environmental disruption was concern over a newly publicized 'welfare gap' (*fukushi gappu*). Government expenditure on social welfare was found to be woefully inadequate—not much more in per capita outlay each year than in Tunisia and Ceylon—and the consequences of low spending on social overheads were widely lamented. Only 13 per cent of Japanese roads were paved at the time, and a high proportion of streets lacked sidewalks to provide pedestrians with some protection from vehicular traffic. Owing in large measure to the inadequacy of sewerage systems, only 17.1 per cent of Japanese dwellings were equipped with flush toilets. In Japanese cities the area of park space per capita lagged far behind the cities of the West, and other recreational facilities were in short supply. Tokyo, to cite an extreme example, had only 1.2 square meters of park space per capita, compared to 14.4 square meters in West Berlin, 19 in New York City, and 22.8 in London. Of a total of 18,563 indoor sports centers in Japan in 1971, only 357 were open to the public; only 729 of the 8,897 swimming pools in the country were public.

Housing and land prices first surfaced as a major issue in these same years. In Tokyo and Osaka, for example, the cost of building a small house with 62 square meters of floor space was found to have almost doubled between 1950 and 1971, while the cost of purchasing the 103 square meters of land to build it on had increased twentyfold. Commuting times for employees in both rented and owner-occupied accommodation increased as people flocked to the suburbs to find affordable living space. The average white-collar employee might well leave home in the morning before his children woke up and return home after they had gone to bed. At the weekend, he often slept during the day to recover from the stress not only of long hours on the job but also of getting to and from his place of work. Housewives began to complain of the isolation they felt during the day, when their children were off at school and their husbands far away at work, in the hastily constructed and generally poorly provisioned bedroom communities they inhabited. Men began to die of overwork (*karōshi*).[6]

When a Ministry of Agriculture survey indicated that cadmium effluents were poisoning rice crops elsewhere than in Toyama Prefecture, the original site of *itai itai* disease, Araki Masuo, former chairman of the National Public Safety Commission and Director-General of the Administrative Agency, urged his constituents in Kyushu to 'have the spirit to eat contaminated rice'.[7] This resounding call for renewed commitment to the production-first policies of the past two decades, no matter what the cost, did not have the desired effect on his audience, and rather than the compliance he appears to have expected, Araki met with criticism for his acute insensitivity. His experience was not unusual.

The celebrated plan of Tanaka Kakuei (prime minister, 1972–4) to 'remodel the Japanese archipelago' by, among other things, diffusing industry more evenly throughout the country, met with considerable resistance from the inhabitants of relatively unspoiled regions beyond the industrial heartland of Japan, who did not wish the newly revealed and much-publicized problems of that heartland visited upon them. Nor were they keen to endure the noise and other health hazards of high-speed 'bullet' trains in (literally) their own backyards. Plans to reclaim shoreline for the construction of several large-scale coastal industrial complexes had to be curtailed in the face of local opposition, as for a time were plans to extend the high-speed rail network beyond the newly opened Tokaido route.

During 1973 fishermen in several water-zones of the country blockaded the entrances to harbors used by firms thought to be responsible for pollution. In some instances they also plugged the outlets for waste water from firms using mercury as a catalyst in producing acetoaldehyde, caustic soda, or vinyl chloride, causing the firms to suspend operations for a time. In July of that year thousands of fishermen gathered in Tokyo for a protest rally. In addition to the usual noisy street demonstrations, they lobbied Keidanren (the influential Federation of Economic Organizations), demanding that enterprises 'awake to their social responsibility for environmental protection'.[8]

This demand, and similar demands from the large number of local citizens' action groups organized in the late 1960s and early 1970s to protest against a veritable host of perceived defects in the *status quo*, seemed to some observers to spell the end of the ascendancy of the Liberal Democratic Party (LDP), which had governed Japan since 1955. Disaffection with its pro-business, unrestricted growth policies, it was argued, had reached a peak. Already voters in a number of communities had elected independent or left-wing assemblymen committed to fighting pollution, and reformist mayors representing the Socialist and Communist Parties had taken office in five of Japan's major cities, including Tokyo. The LDP would be toppled from below, losing first its control of the prefectures and then its control of the nation. With its fall from power, the economic goals it had championed without interruption since 1955 would be cast aside. A new Japan, under new leadership and committed to providing all of its citizens with a decent quality of life, would emerge.

As we know, the key element in this scenario was not realized: the LDP retained control of the lower house of the Diet until 1993. But this did not mean that concern over the quality of life was ignored. Far from it. Integral to the LDP's continued ascendancy was its ability—aided and abetted (even nudged in important ways) by the bureaucracy—to respond to popular concern, at least to a politically meaningful degree.

The Araki Masuos of the party, who advocated growth at any cost, were muzzled and much attention paid to the articulation of views on food safety and other problems which the Japanese public would accept. By the mid-1970s a variety of anti-pollution laws had been passed by the Diet. Polluting industries found themselves on the defensive, subjected to heavy penalties in a number of court cases that were decided against them, and denied the protection to which they had become accustomed over the years from such key bodies as the Ministry of International Trade and Industry. From 1973, widely hailed as 'the dawn of welfare provision' (*fukushi gannen*), a series of carefully calibrated steps were taken by the government to bring state expenditure on social security and health care up to 'proper' Western European levels. The word 'social' entered the lexicon of the Economic Planning Agency, and new national plans for the creation of an environmentally sensitive, welfare-oriented postindustrial economy, based on clean, knowledge-intensive industries, were published apace.

To be sure, new legislation and new national plans did not in themselves suffice to bring about radical change in actual business practice. Had it not been for the first oil crisis of 1973, which demonstrated to industry as well as to government in Japan that the world market for natural resources was no longer a buyer's market and that a rethinking of Japanese economic policy was essential, little more than lip service might have been paid to growing public discontent. In this sense, the oil crisis came to the LDP's (and Japan's) rescue, by forcing politicians, bureaucrats, and industrialists alike to think seriously about a new economic future for the country. That the use of fuel oil in the production of Japanese steel fell from 128 kiloliters per ton in 1973 to 86 kiloliters in 1979 was the result, I would argue, of market forces, not of the steel industry's anxiety over atmospheric pollution in the vicinity of its mills. But fall it did, as did the consumption of energy in other industrial processes and products. New economic realities meant that the economy's reliance on natural resources must diminish and that the Japanese growth machine must slow.

Simultaneously, the first oil crisis and the severe recession it induced gave renewed credence to the establishment's portrayal of the Japanese economy as inherently fragile—according to this view, Japan was only a small island country (*semai shimaguni*), highly dependent on trade and hence on events elsewhere over which Japan could have no control—and public demands for immediate economic and social reforms abated somewhat during the remainder of the 1970s. As a result of the LDP's ability to shift course, and of an economic climate that gave it the precious time it needed to make that shift, its political ascendancy was maintained. But public sensitivity to both environmental disruption and the welfare gap remained a force to be reckoned with thereafter. Although not as prominent in public discourse as in the early 1970s, concern with the quality of life in Japan lay just beneath the surface of media and popular attention, ready to erupt at the slightest hint of yet another pollution or welfare 'scandal'.

8 | Japanese Society in the Early 1990s

When most Westerners think of Japan, they think of vast, densely populated cities. Teeming masses of men in dark suits crowd on to commuter trains early each morning, en route from their tiny flats (euphemistically known as *manshon*, from the English word mansion) to gleaming office towers of glass and steel, where they spend long hours planning yet new inroads into beleaguered foreign markets for the goods their companies manufacture. Identically dressed young men exercise and sing lustily in unison in the car parks of the huge factories where they are employed for life, before going indoors to tend the robots that dominate the production lines. Unsmiling teenagers sit in the serried rows of cram schools (*juku*) at night, furiously taking notes on the facts that will help them pass entrance examinations to secondary schools and universities. Slim, well-dressed housewives shepherd their uniformed infants to kindergarten along busy city streets and shop for the latest in fashions and sophisticated consumer goods in opulently appointed department stores. Over 90 per cent of these people belong to the middle class; they agree on most things, and they subordinate themselves to collective goals to an extent unparalleled in any Western society.

Based largely on impressions of metropolitan Tokyo, the nation's economic as well as political capital, and to a lesser extent on impressions of Osaka, the nation's third largest city, this image is also an extrapolation from the contact most Westerners have with Japan, indirectly via its leading exports. To the extent that, say, automobiles and personal stereos of Japanese manufacture impinge upon us, we see Japan in their terms. These items certainly exist, people (and a goodly number of robots) produce them in high-tech factories and companies go to considerable lengths to sell them to us, but this represents only a tiny fraction of national life. Indeed, even Tokyo and Osaka are rather poorly described by the prevailing image of Japan.

Most Japanese of working age are employed in the service sector of the economy, not in manufacturing, and over 40 per cent of all those going to work each day are women, including a high proportion of married women who must find time for housework and shopping for the essentials of daily life at night and at weekends. Over 93 per cent of all business establishments are small, with fewer than ten employees. Even within the manufacturing sector small firms with from four to ninety-nine employees predominate and together account for roughly 55 per cent of employment in the sector and a significant share in total value-added (37.1 per cent) and total shipments of manufactured goods (32.9 per cent). Most industrial production is aimed at the domestic market, and a wide array of fairly mundane items—soap powders and toothpaste, paper clips and pencils—are produced in addition to the more glamorous items we tend to associate with Japan.

A substantial number of teenagers do not attend cram schools, and while about half of all high-school graduates now take the highly competitive entrance examinations for college or university places, the other half do not. The average floor space per dwelling in Japan is somewhat larger than in Belgium, although the average floor space per person is about 9 per cent less. As we shall see, access to affordable housing even approximating the national average in size and quality is a problem in Tokyo and other densely populated metropolitan areas, but the residents here and elsewhere of *manshon* are not the victims of advertising sleaze or false consciousness: the term refers not to palatial dwellings, but to the purpose-built mansion blocks of apartments constructed in London and other British cities in the late nineteenth and early twentieth centuries, primarily for members of the burgeoning urban middle class, which were the inspiration for much urban housing in postwar Japan.

It is to some form of middling lifestyle not to middle-class membership that about 90 per cent of Japanese associate *themselves* in annual public opinion surveys. If one takes a closer look at the six categories into which their replies are placed—upper, upper-middling, middle-middling, lower-middling, lower, don't know—the second through fourth of which are totaled to yield the widely reported 'middle class' result, only about 54 per cent, probably close to the norm for any developed society in the late twentieth century, see themselves as middle-middling. If one applies such widely used distinctions of social status or class membership as educational attainment, type of employment, income level, property ownership, and social influence to the objective data that are also available, a much more familiar pattern of stratification emerges. Indeed, the gap between rich and poor, the advantaged and disadvantaged, within Japan may well be widening, as the children of parents with the highest incomes continue to do proportionately better than others in securing the educational credentials that provide access to high-income futures and as property ownership becomes increasingly skewed. The Japanese disagree among themselves about all sorts of things, and competition among individuals within the same school, neighborhood, or work group and between such groups commonly occurs, indeed it is often encouraged by those in positions of authority within the groups.

Without doubt, a massive increase in the share of the population living in urban areas has occurred in Japan since the end of the Second World War, most of it having taken place by 1970 (Table 1). In 1950, the majority of Japanese still lived in towns and villages; there were 248 cities, four of which had populations of over 1 million, but collectively these were home to only a little over one-third of all Japanese. In 1970, this distribution had been reversed, and well over two-thirds of all Japanese lived in cities, of which there were now 579, including eight with populations of

Table 1. *Population by place of residence, 1950–1990* (%)

	1950	1970	1990
In cities	**37.4**	**72.1**	**77.4**
1,000,000+ inhabitants	11.4	20.1	20.5
100,000–999,999 inhabitants	14.2	31.5	38.1
under 100,000 inhabitants	11.8	20.5	18.8
In towns and villages	**62.6**	**27.9**	**22.6**
10,000+ inhabitants	16.5	18.6	15.7
under 10,000 inhabitants	46.1	9.3	6.9

Sources: *Sūji de miru Nihon no hyakunen* (Kokuseisha, 1986); Statistics Bureau, Management and Coordination Agency, *Japan Statistical Yearbook* (1992).

over 1 million. In 1990, the number of cities had increased to 656, eleven of which had populations of over 1 million, and the proportion of urban residents within the total population of slightly over 123 million had increased to over 77 per cent. The typical residents of Japan today are indeed city dwellers, but the urban environments they inhabit vary considerably in scale as well in diversity of employment, range of cultural amenities, and living costs. It should be noted that roughly the same number of people live in the 447 cities with populations of less than 100,000 as live in the eleven with more than 1 million, and the greatest number live in cities that are between these two extremes in size. Even the eleven largest cities differ markedly from one another in many respects—with, for example, the average commuting time per day for employees working in Sapporo or Nagoya only about half that prevailing in Tokyo. To a greater extent than may be the case with other capital cities, Tokyo is best thought of as exceptional, not only in its size and its influence both nationally and internationally, but also in its problems.

As shown in Table 2, the shift of population to cities has been accompanied—indeed induced—by shifts in employment opportunities. By 1970 the secondary and tertiary sectors of the economy had far outstripped the primary sector as loci of employment for those of working age, and the Japanese had become a nation predominately of employees in industrial and service occupa-

Table 2. *Labor force by sector and employment status, 1950–1990* (%)

	1950	1970	1990
By Sector			
Primary	48.3	19.3	7.2
Secondary	21.9	34.1	33.8
Tertiary	29.7	46.5	59.0
By Status			
Self-employed	26.2	19.2	14.1
Family worker	34.4	15.8	8.3
Employee	39.3	64.9	77.6

Sources: As in Table 1.

tions. Even in 1990, however, Japan retained a fairly large stratum of self-employed and family workers, rivaled only by Italy among the leading seven OECD economies. If one eliminates (predominantly unpaid) family workers and considers the self-employed alone, the rate in Japan is almost identical to that in Britain, and as in Britain self-employment ranges from the many proprietors of small retail shops and restaurants to the very few owners of large concerns.

Despite some narrowing since the 1960s of the gap in basic pay and benefits provided to employees by the relatively few large firms and the many small ones, it is still possible to divide employees into three distinct groups on the basis of earnings, non-monetary rewards, and job security: (1) a minority of both shop-floor and administrative personnel, perhaps a quarter to a third of all employees, who are full-time, regular, and on the whole permanent members of large enterprises, better paid than almost all other employees, and eligible for the full range of corporate welfare facilities; (2) a not-insignificant number of non-member temporary, seasonal, or part-time employees of large enterprises, who receive lower wages and reduced access to benefits and who can be and are dismissed when it is in the firm's interests to cut labor costs; and (3) a substantial number, probably the majority of all employees, again including both shop-floor and administrative personnel, who are full-time, seasonal, or part-time employees of small enterprises, earn less than their counterparts in large firms and change employers (both voluntarily and involuntarily) at rates that approximate those prevailing in labor markets in the West.

The employees of small firms tend to work longer scheduled hours than do those in large firms, and hence to earn less in overtime pay. The semi-annual bonuses they receive, which make up a larger share of total earnings in Japan than elsewhere, generally are less than half those paid by large firms. The sums their employers spend per employee on benefits, including mandatory health insurance and pension payments, are considerably lower than in large firms. In the mid-1980s, and in manufacturing industries alone, workers in small firms with fewer than 100 employees earned 55 per cent of the incomes of workers in firms with 1,000 or more employees, compared to 73 per cent in Britain, 70 per cent in France or Italy, and 66 per cent in the United States. The average annual earnings of women in full-time employment are about 55 per cent those of men, primarily because these women tend to have less seniority than their male colleagues and to work for smaller firms. That a high proportion of women in the labor force are employed part-time, which in Japan can mean anything up to about 35 hours per week, reduces the average annual earnings of all women employees to an even lower level.[1]

The Western image of Japan is of a predominantly youthful country, save perhaps for its political leaders, and this too is at variance with reality. Well over 60 per cent of all Japanese have been born since the end of the Second World War, but that war ended half a century ago and the baby boom that followed it was repeated, on a considerably reduced scale, only once when the baby boomers themselves produced children in the 1970s. As in other developed countries, although at what appears to be a particularly rapid rate, Japanese society is aging, or 'greying'. The shockwaves this demographic reality have been sending through the system since the late 1970s cannot be overestimated. Who will fill the jobs that have hitherto relied on young, relatively

Table 3. *Age distribution, 1950–2010 (%)*

	1950	1970	1990	2010*
Aged 0–14	35.4	23.9	18.2	16.4
Aged 15–64	59.7	69.0	69.7	62.5
Aged 65+	4.9	7.1	12.1	21.1
Total population in millions	83.2	103.7	123.6	129.4

*Projected figures for 2010.

Sources: As in Table 1.

inexpensive labor? How will those of working age cope with the tax burden needed to finance education for the young and, more urgently, medical and welfare services for the elderly? Can a way be found to induce the Japanese, and Japanese women in particular, to increase the national birthrate and/or to assume even greater responsibility for care of the old and infirm?

As shown in Table 3, the percentage of Japanese aged 14 or under has nearly halved since 1950, while the percentage of those over the age of 65 has more than doubled. By the year 2010, when its population reaches a projected peak of 129 million, Japan will face an almost rectangular age 'pyramid', with the prospect for over a decade to come of a declining population of working-age adults to sustain an already large and rapidly expanding population of the elderly and a relatively small and still declining population of the very young.

Almost a quarter of those over the age of 65 (36 per cent of men and 10 per cent of women) are still in work, and collectively they form almost 6 per cent of the total labor force. Of those in self-employment, some farm the land and many others operate small retail shops. Of those who are employees, not a few have taken a downward step in pay and responsibilities after formal retirement at 60 (up from 55, the retirement age originally set in 1902) to eke out their pensions with temporary jobs with their former employers or in other, typically smaller, enterprises. In the 1930s the average life expectancy of Japanese men was roughly 50 years, 5 years *below* the then retirement age; it is now over 76 years (and over 82 years for women), roughly 16 years *above* retirement age. Coping with life after the end of earnings or of peak earnings has become an increasingly serious problem for older Japanese and for their children.

It would take at least another book and far more expertise than I possess to discuss every aspect of contemporary Japanese society in adequate detail. Instead, I propose to focus in the remainder of this chapter on just three topics: the present situation of and future prospects for farmers, the status and concerns of women, and the current social-management strategies of the state. As will soon become apparent, these topics are not as unrelated as they might at first appear.

Farmers and Farming in Today's Japan

To apply a trenchant observation made by Sir George Sansom about the ruling élite of Tokugawa Japan to a radically different context, the urban majority of Japan today '[think] highly of agriculture, but not of agriculturalists'.[2] At a pragmatic level, most urban residents accept the argument that the domestic farming sector protects them to a degree from the consequences of relatively low rates of national self-sufficiency in food (under 50 per cent on a calorie basis). Foodstuffs generally rank as the third most important item, by value, in Japanese imports, and ever since the US government imposed a sudden embargo on soy-bean exports in 1973, largely for domestic reasons, the Japanese have been sensitive not only to the risks of undue reliance on any single trading partner for commodities in this area but also to the possibility of a global crisis in food supplies. In the latter event, whether of climatic, economic, or political origin, they would no longer be able to sustain the high dietary standard they have achieved by trade, but they would still have enough rice, potatoes, and vegetables, and almost enough eggs and dairy products, from domestic sources to keep them alive. Most urban residents also believe, despite some evidence to the contrary, that the domestic farming sector provides them with food that not only is fresher, but also safer from contamination by dangerous chemicals than their imported counterparts.

These pragmatic considerations are reinforced—perhaps even outweighed in some quarters—by considerations of an ideological nature. As in many other countries within the developed world, agriculture and rural life in Japan have become idealized as the source of basic values and national character the more remote from the direct experience of the non-agricultural majority they have grown. In the Japanese case, it is the particular characteristics of one crop, short-grain paddy rice of the japonica type, and of the communities of farmers which evolved to grow it in ancient times, that infuse the ideal and define the culture. The crop required collective effort in the creation and maintenance of local irrigation systems, in transplanting young rice seedlings, and in bringing in the harvest field by field, and that is portrayed as the source of the unique spirit of solidarity and co-operation among the Japanese people in modern times. To maintain agriculture and rural ways is to retain an essential link with tradition and to provide a continuing (and, some members of the establishment would say, increasingly necessary) inspiration to younger generations.

As discussed previously, Japan underwent an earlier round of such rural myth-making during the interwar era, but then most people still had some connection with farming, and their responses to the rhetoric of officials and others were tempered by awareness of the harsher realities of rural life, which they themselves experienced or from which they had only recently escaped. Now there is virtually nothing to restrain their imaginations—except, that is, for the agriculturalists who produce the crops and inhabit the villages of Japan today. Farmers are disliked by urban Japanese, mostly because insufficient numbers of them are seen to live up to the idyll of the countryside and because some farmers (fewer by far than generally assumed) have become exceedingly wealthy by virtue of selling land in the path of expanding cities. It is one thing for the urban majority to be called upon to support domestic farming with a share of their taxes and with the high prices they must pay for many domestically produced food items, but it is another to be expected to support farmers who blot the lush, green landscape of the countryside with paved roads, noisy machinery, seemingly endless thermoplastic tunnels for vegetable crops, large metal structures for mushroom factories, and other unsightly, small-scale agro-industrial ventures, not to mention new houses even larger and often more modern than those in affluent city suburbs.

The urban majority may well have good reason to be concerned about the financial burdens imposed on them in sustaining Japanese agriculture, but their identification of the villains of the piece is largely misplaced. The problem is, at root, one of policy not persons, and can be traced back to the land reform carried out during the postwar Occupation.

Widely regarded as one of the most successful of Occupation reforms, the postwar land reform virtually eliminated farm tenancy in Japan. Absentee landlords were compelled to sell their entire holdings of arable land to the state at 1945 prices; resident landlords were allowed to retain no more than about 7 acres of arable land on average (about 29 acres in Hokkaido, where dairy farming prevailed), provided they were willing and able to farm at least two-thirds of the acreage themselves; and the relatively small number of owner-cultivators with holdings above the permitted ceilings were also required, in most cases, to sell their surplus acreage. The land thus acquired by the state was resold primarily to existing tenant farmers at the same 1945 prices, with low-interest loans and runaway inflation during the late 1940s making their payment for it relatively easy; subsequent land transfers were subject to approval by local land committees and, ultimately, by the prefectural government. By 1950, when the reform was substantially completed, some 90 per cent of all arable land (roughly double the rate prevailing since the early 1900s) was owned by those who cultivated it. Rents on the 10 per cent or so of land that remained in tenancy were made payable in cash at moderate levels, and security of tenure assured. All farmers were encouraged to join newly 'democratized' agricultural co-operatives, although the permitted activities of the latter were confined to credit, purchasing, and marketing; co-operative production was rejected by the Occupation as socialistic.

The land reform was a notable achievement, certainly less sullied in its implementation by vested interests than many other attempts in the early postwar era or since elsewhere in the world, but it must be recognized that it did not address the basic structural defect that had afflicted Japanese agriculture for decades: the scarcity of arable land in relation to the number of farm households. The emphasis of the reform was on the elimination of a problem, tenancy, which was portrayed more than a little simplistically within the central headquarters of the Occupation as a major source of Japanese militarism and aggression in the 1930s, and not on the creation of an economically efficient agricultural sector. One need not accept *in toto* the reading of recent Japanese history which infused the reform to appreciate that no viable alternative to its thrust existed at the time. As noted earlier, Japan lay prostrate in defeat, its major cities in ruins, many of its factories idle, and its rural population swelled by urban refugees. There was no place at the time for 'excess' farmers to go, nor any likelihood of alternative full-time employment for them in the near future. As a result, the available land was redistributed among all of those who qualified (or who could manage, with some benign connivance, on the part of their neighbors, to qualify) as cultivators, and some 6 million farm households ended up cultivating some 6 million *chō* of land, or about 2.45 acres each on average. Some households were able to lay claim to more acreage, up to the permitted local ceiling; well over one-third ended up with less than an acre, and only about a half emerged with enough land, the area of which varied by region and cropping pattern, to support themselves by farming alone. To the extent that economic considerations played a part in the reform, these manifested themselves in the expectation that pride of ownership and price supports would stimulate farmers to boost output. Their incomes would increase, bringing an end to rural poverty, and the nation would be fed, thus relieving the United States of the burden of massive food aid to its former enemy.

The Japanese government ratified the land reform in 1952, just after the Occupation ended, and continued to enforce its provisions on the permissible scale of rural land ownership and the leasing of farmland, as well as maintaining price supports for certain key crops, chief among them rice, and imposing quotas or other restrictions on certain agricultural imports. That electoral politics came to play an important part in the design and operation of these policies cannot be denied (from the mid-1950s onward the ruling Liberal Democratic Party relied heavily on rural votes, which counted for far more than urban votes in the absence of meaningful redistricting, and went to considerable lengths to curry favor within the countryside[3]) but a broader and more noble agenda was also followed. Land reforms need time— at least a generation, it would appear from examples around the world—to solidify, before market forces can once again be freely unleashed and the probable reconcentration of land in the hands of those who can make the most of it for agricultural or other purposes, as opposed to those whose families merely used to control it, can be allowed to occur. The closing of a sizable income gap between the typical residents of both countryside and city by means of price supports and other assistance to farmers not only did much to balance the books of history, in the sense that resources which had earlier been extracted from the countryside to help finance Japan's industrialization were now ploughed back into it, it also created millions of new consumers for the products of Japanese industry and helped to reduce the country's reliance on export sales. The diffusion rate of most durable consumer goods, from refrigerators and washing machines to color television sets and microwave ovens, has been virtually identical in countryside and city in recent years, and a higher percentage of rural Japanese have purchased automobiles and motor scooters than have their (admittedly far more numerous) urban counterparts. Irritating though it may have become to many city dwellers, the increased affluence of farmers has proved a joy to domestic manufacturers.

Working within the contours of the land reform while at the same time promoting the development of agriculture required a delicate and increasingly problematic balancing act for bureaucrats, however, especially those within the Ministry of Agriculture, Forestry, and Fisheries (MAFF). Rapid economic growth during the 'miracle' years did create far more new job opportunities in the non-agricultural sector far more quickly than

Occupation officials had anticipated, and for the first time in Japan's modern history an absolute decrease occurred in the number of farm households, from about 6 million in 1950 to 5.3 million in 1970 and 4.5 million in the early 1980s. Largely on the basis of this evolving trend and its reading of Japan's food-security needs in future, MAFF committed itself in 1961 to the promotion of 'viable family farming', that is, to households whose members were fully engaged in agriculture on holdings of a size that would permit economies of scale and provide incomes comparable to those of average urban workers.

This objective assumed, unduly optimistically as it turned out, that most of the farm households with very small holdings would soon leave agriculture altogether for more remunerative employment elsewhere and that the land they owned would pass into the hands of their more substantial neighbors. Only to a limited extent did this occur. A more significant trend, already observable by the late 1950s, was the increase in the number of part-time farm households. These were of two general types, those whose family income from agriculture exceeded income from non-agricultural sources and those whose non-agricultural income exceeded agricultural income. In 1950, the farming population as a whole was evenly split between full-time and part-time households, and there was a rough parity in number between the two types of part-time farm families; at a time when the economy was still reeling from the effects of the war, full-time farm families generally were better off economically than part-timers of either type. By 1970, the situation was radically different. Full-time farm households had fallen to 15 per cent of the total and only about half of them could be considered 'viable'; the other half, not infrequently consisting of an elderly couple, were struggling to make a go of it on holdings well below 'optimum' size or efficiency. Part-time farm households of the second type, those depending mainly on non-agricultural work, were not only the most numerous, at slightly over 50 per cent of all farm households, but also, in income terms, the most prosperous, even though they generally owned very little land. At first, their prosperity was achieved by leaving farming to the wives and grandparents within the family while the male househead and one or more of his adult children went off to work in factories or on construction sites. Later it was achieved by the purchase of machinery which made it possible for the househead to carry out most farming tasks, especially those related to the cultivation of rice, at the weekend, allowing him, any of his adult children who remained in residence, and, increasingly, his wife and/or daughter-in-law, to pursue other work on weekdays. Primarily because of steadily increasing official rice prices and the absence of any limit to the volume the government would buy from farmers, rice became the preferred crop of these part-time 'weekend' farmers. What they produced was not of particularly high quality, but that did not matter, as the state would buy all that they did not need for their own consumption at prices that soon surpassed those of imported rice.

Rice became a useful little earner for these farmers, even as the dietary habits of the majority of Japanese began to change and rice consumption nationwide began to decline. Surplus stocks of rice started to mount, as did the financial burden on the state, and on taxpayers. An advertising campaign launched by the nationwide Union of Agricultural Co-operatives (Nōkyō) in the early 1980s to boost domestic rice consumption was notable for its ingenuity, but not for its impact. Although urban Japanese were assured that a bowl or two of steaming hot rice for breakfast would give them more of the energy they needed for a hard day's work than toast and eggs, and women were advised that the more highly polished white rice they consumed the paler and more beautiful their complexions would become, per capita annual rice consumption continued to decline. Roughly 115 kilograms per person in 1960, it had fallen to only 70 kilograms in 1989.

Clearly, something had gone awry with official plans for the future of Japanese agriculture, and a prolonged and complicated effort to rectify the situation commenced. In the process, much blame was attributed in the media to farmers, particularly those with tiny holdings of land, for their refusal to bow to the economic realities of their situation, sell their land, and move to towns or cities. The innate attachment of peasants to the land and, somewhat contradictorily, the speculative instincts of the owners of real estate that might eventually be sold at great profit for factory or housing sites were decried, and little attention paid to the real obstacles to selling out and moving on that most part-time farmers faced: the uncertainty of their continued employment in the volatile small industrial sector, where many of them had secured work; the preference of larger, more stable enterprises for young workers of school-leaving age; the relatively early retirement age for employees in all non-agricultural enterprises; the low level of state social-security benefits then available; and the higher costs of urban housing and urban life in general. Until the government relaxed its vigilance over the resurgence of rural landlordism, it was risky to lease even a portion of one's holding to other farmers, especially if one would be moving away from the community and becoming an absentee owner. So long as small factories and other enterprises continued to sprout up in rural districts, often with the encouragement of local politicians, and to provide employment however low paid in relation to employment in larger enterprises, it made sense to continue living in the house one already owned, to commute to work and to hang on to the land, however small and poorly cared for it might be, that could provide food for the family now and in the future. If, at the same time, one child could be induced to follow the same route, there would be someone on hand to provide care when work of any kind was no longer possible, and the tragedy of a lonely, destitute death would be avoided.

Securing a successor, ideally a son who was willing to take responsibility for the family and its land in future, increasingly became a concern for all farmers, whether part- or full-time. Indeed, full-time farmers often experienced the greater difficulty in this respect, for MAFF's vision of viable family farming in which *all* family members played an active role did not necessarily suit the ambitions of young women of rural origin. Owing in large measure to the expanded educational opportunities available to them in the postwar era and the images of 'modern Japan' they picked up from all those rural television sets, as well as to the laments heard from their mothers about subordination to the mothers-in law who ran the households young brides joined or about the necessity of neglecting the needs of children to attend to essential chores, many young women came to resist the idea of marrying a farmer and dedicating themselves to an 'old-fashioned' life of toil. It was one thing for a farmer's son to weigh the alternatives and opt for succession; it was another for him to consign himself to lifelong bachelorhood in the process. The boom in house construction in rural areas from the late 1960s onward was primarily a response to this situation—separate and well-equipped quarters for a newly married successor couple figured prominently in most such projects—as was the investment by greater numbers of full-time farmers in labor-saving machinery, so that young brides could devote more of their time to homemaking, child care, and, eventually, to 'dignified' non-agricultural employment.

Full-time farmers, too, came to welcome the location of small, non-agricultural enterprises in the surrounding countryside, precisely because they made a local marriage more attractive to local girls. Despite such efforts, however, not all younger farmers were able to secure local or even Japanese brides, and some among them—especially those who lived in villages at a considerable remove from the highways or rail links that factories and other non-agricultural enterprises required—found it necessary to look farther afield, to the Philippines in particular, for partners to share their lives. Some years before 'internationalization' (*kokusaika*) became a buzzword among urban élites, Japanese farmers had undertaken pioneering efforts in that direction.

Of course, the efforts of these farmers were limited to the marriage market, not to the international market-place in agricultural commodities. To the governments of a number of countries which sought during the 1970s and early 1980s to increase their agricultural exports to Japan as a means of countering mounting bilateral trade deficits, criticisms of the protection afforded to Japanese agriculture began to loom ever larger in their dealings with the nation's leadership in Tokyo. As on a number of other issues, this foreign pressure (*gaiatsu*) gave impetus to domestic criticisms of existing policies and practices and, ultimately, proved useful in justifying reforms 'in the larger interests of the nation as a whole' that would impinge in unsettling ways on certain segments of the population.

The culminating events in this particular exposure to *gaiatsu* were the Uruguay Round of multilateral trade talks within GATT (1987–93) and the decisions by the Japanese government in the early 1990s to end quotas on imported citrus fruits and beef and—most dramatically, so far as media coverage in Japan and the West was concerned—to permit the importing of substantial quantities of foreign rice. For over two decades, however, Japanese agricultural policies had been changing in subtle and not-so-subtle ways, as MAFF, with no little input from other ministries and even with some support from the more demographically realistic politicians within the LDP, sought to steer the agricultural sector and at least some of the nation's farmers toward an economically sustainable future.

This process had begun in the late 1960s with the provision of incentives to farmers, in the form of special subsidies and the lure of sales at premium prices, to grow higher quality, 'brand-name' rice—a measure which left weekend farmers at a disadvantage, at least initially, because higher quality rice required more care than they could provide. It was followed, in 1971, by a much-heralded program to pay farmers for leaving some of their rice paddies fallow or planting crops such as wheat instead of rice, and, at roughly the same time, by a little-noticed policy to encourage the very producers' co-operatives the Occupation had found so objectionable, in order that some economies of scale even without transfers of land ownership could be achieved.

Efforts to encourage diversification away from rice continued throughout the 1970s and early 1980s, climaxing in 1987 (largely at the insistence of the Ministry of Finance) in the first-ever drop in the official rice price paid to producers since the 1950s, and the maintenance of generally stable or declining producers' prices thereafter. Finally, as part of a more general land tax reform approved by the Diet in 1991 to curb speculation and steep rises in land prices in or near large cities, radical changes were effected in the taxation of farmland located within designated 'urbanization promotion areas' in the Tokyo, Nagoya, and Osaka metropolitan regions. Exemption from inheritance tax on such farmland was abolished, and the fixed assets tax collected by municipalities was to be levied at the markedly higher rate for residential land. Only by having their holdings designated as 'productive green areas' could farmers in these areas continue to pay fixed asset taxes at the lower farmland rate, but the land could not subsequently be converted to non-agricultural use unless all the exempted taxes were paid. As the legislation intended, most farmers opted to pay tax at the residential rate in order to avoid any restriction on its future use, and many of them began to sell all or part of their holdings.

The interests of foreigners—in the form of protests over the exorbitant cost of securing business premises in metropolitan Japan—played only a minor role in the latter measure. Domestic protests over the high cost of urban land for housing and social infrastructure, as well as the concern in some quarters that a 'widened asset gap could damage people's fundamental trust in equality of opportunity and lead to a decline in the will to work and the business spirit',[4] clearly were of greater importance. Much the same conclusion can be drawn, I think, about the earlier measures to which I have referred. These were the product of a primarily internal debate, certainly not without parallel elsewhere in the developed world, over the extent to which domestic agriculture should remain eligible for 'special' treatment in an otherwise fairly competitive and overwhelmingly urban economic environment. Over time, MAFF was constrained to move toward deregulation and the phased but nonetheless significant unleashing of market forces within the countryside. In effect, by the early 1990s, the era of the land reform had come to an end, along with, more broadly, the saliency of the memories of food shortages, which had shaped agricultural policy in all of the countries involved in the Second World War. Foreign pressure served to bring this denouement about somewhat more quickly and definitively—and possibly at less electoral risk to Japanese politicians—than might otherwise have been the case.

It remains to be seen just how, and how many, Japanese farmers adjust to the new 'market-adaptable' approach they are now being called upon to pursue. Even before the formal ending of the Uruguay Round, the pace of retreat from farming nationwide had accelerated dramatically, from an average decrease of 40,000 per year in the number of farm households during the 1980s to almost 360,000 in 1990 alone and a further decrease of 900,000 in 1991. Only 2.9 million farm households remained in 1991, down from 4.5 million roughly a decade earlier, and they were, except for the very old among their ranks, a leaner and fitter lot. Many marginal operators, who had been highly dependent on price supports of one kind or another, had given up, as had others whose land lay within the urbanization promotion areas of Greater Tokyo, Nagoya, and Osaka. While some farmers in picturesque mountain villages had found a niche for themselves in the fairly new 'tourist agriculture' industry, attracting urban visitors in search of a meaningful rural experience, the balance had shifted to farmers in the many basins and plains to the north, west, and south of the major metropolitan regions, where agriculture remained important to the local economy and potentially profitable in future. Their numbers, too, are apt to decline in the years ahead, but this will not necessarily lead to the decline of part-time farming in these districts or to a dramatic increase by means of land purchases in the scale of local full-time farm operations. A multiplicity of trends, varying from district to district, appears more likely in the medium term.

Of the 2.9 million farm households nationwide in 1991, part-time farm households of the second type (those earning more from non-agricultural activity than from farming) constituted roughly 70 per cent of the total, and they predominated, too, within most of the major agricultural districts of the country. Even MAFF has now accepted their existence, at least for the time being. Its efforts focus on promoting improvements in the productivity and management—especially by means of co-operatives and other organizations—of regional agriculture as a whole, regardless of the income profiles of local farmers. Only in part can this be seen as a concession to the interests of Japanese manufacturing, which might have located more of its subcontracting or food-processing operations offshore if it could not obtain relatively inexpensive labor in the countryside at home; it is also a response to the concerns and the behavior of farmers over the past thirty years or so, as they attempted to cope in diverse ways with the opportunities and problems they themselves perceived. That diversity is now accepted by the officials responsible for agricultural policy, and part-time farmers are welcome to join their full-time neighbors in the quest for new ways to keep local farming viable. Some may prosper by virtue of their innovative responses to changing consumer demand, while others will go under, either because they fail to innovate or because they do so without success.

Much the same uncertain fate awaits the minority of full-time farmers. Some of those who produce brand-name rice, which as of 1992 accounted for over 70 per cent of all Japanese rice traded, may be able to expand their operations (chauvinistic hyperbole aside, the best Japanese rice is indeed superior in taste to anything of the japonica type that farmers in California, Australia, or Thailand can produce and will continue to sell at a premium within Japan) but even those farmers in the most favored rice-producing districts, where the days are warm and the nights cool during the growing season, will need to diversify to an extent to avoid the risks of monoculture, and not all of their ventures will pay off.

Eventually, after a period of experimentation and flux, it may be that traditional land-dependent crops, such as rice and soy beans, prove less profitable than such 'high-tech', land-saving operations as hydroponics or other forms of factory agriculture, in which case the successful farmer of the future may have an even smaller holding than at present. Indeed, to the extent that farmers can exchange their khaki work clothes for white lab coats and replace the manual labor they now perform with the running of sophisticated biotechnological applications, they may finally be able to solve the problem of succession which has troubled them, and the agricultural sector as a whole, for over thirty years. Young men would want to become farmers again, and young women might well be willing to marry them. Some young women might even be able to qualify as farmers in their own right. As factory farms become discrete enterprises, able to function more or less independently of the communities in which they are located, it could become possible to sell them as going concerns to complete strangers, instead of handing them on to a locally born and bred heir. That would be a truly revolutionary development in the long history of rural Japanese society, and it could begin taking place in at least some agricultural districts within the next few years.

The longer term prospects for Japanese farming are more difficult to assess, as is the case in many Western countries. Public concern with food security and food safety is unlikely to disappear, but if and when reasonably satisfactory regional or even global arrangements for dealing with these matters are in place, public support for any significant degree of food production within Japan could evaporate. There are already those in urban Japan (some industrialists as well as many macroeconomists) who argue that it is high time that Japan cease defying the laws of comparative advantage and consign domestic farming to oblivion. The land thus freed from inefficient production could be used for new factories, new transport systems, and improved housing and recreational facilties for the majority of the population. A few pockets of domestic agriculture might remain, producing crops for the high end of the market, and 'tourist agriculture' might well flourish, but almost all of the nation's food would be acquired from abroad, at lower prices to domestic consumers. If the logic of these arguments, and the mechanisms to make them persuasive to policy-makers, gain force in the decades ahead, Japanese agriculture—and agriculturalists—could well-nigh disappear.

The Status and Concerns of Women

In resisting marriages to local farmers in the early 1960s and beyond, young women of rural origin were seeking to emulate what they saw as the superior lifestyle of their urban counterparts: a home they could call their own from the start of their married life, rather than coresidence with their in-laws, and children to whose nurturing they could devote themselves. That only a small percentage of urban women, principally the wives of managerial personnel in large companies and other members of an emerging new urban middle class,[5] had achieved this lifestyle by the 1960s did not deter them.

Nor were they alone in their aspirations. City girls, too, were susceptible to the appeals of professional domesticity, and marriage to a young man with a secure and adequate income—ideally, a salaried white-collar employee (*sarariiman*) or a skilled shop-floor employee in a large enterprise—became the goal for many of them. As in the United States and much of Europe in the immediate postwar decades, young women embraced marriage and child-rearing as their destiny. In school, girls studied cooking and sewing while boys learned how to use power tools, and in the classes they shared girls generally took care not to outshine the boys. Girls might work for a few years after graduation—after all, the experience could prove useful in snaring an appropriate husband—but to work after marriage in anything other than a family business or an appropriately feminine job such as hairdressing, nursing, or teaching children was viewed as both unnecessary and unwise. To work outside the home after the birth of one's children and before their schooling was well under way was to admit failure in the central purpose of one's life. Only the mavericks within the ranks of young women, those who for one reason or another failed to find a husband, or those who were later widowed or divorced sought careers in employment.

In aspiring to professional domesticity, Japanese girls were not making an autonomous choice, of course. As in other countries emerging from the 'extraordinary' circumstances of the Second World War, they had in most cases been socialized by their parents, by their teachers, and by society at large to accept a highly gendered and not necessarily fully accurate model of peaceful prewar life, which placed them (back) in the home and males out in the workplace and corridors of power. In the Japanese case, this model had its roots in the Meiji era, when the state had proclaimed for all women a role that in essence was based on the idealized division of responsibility within high-status warrior families of the Tokugawa period: women were to be 'good wives and wise mothers' (*ryōsai kenbo*), while their husbands ran the country or, new to the Meiji era, manned its factories.

That most Japanese factories were 'womaned' rather than 'manned' at the time was not allowed to interfere with the propagation of this ideal, and the eagerness of some women in the late nineteenth century to exploit the new opportunities seemingly made possible by the state's commitment to 'civilization and enlightenment' was curtailed. Only men, not women, were allowed to participate in politics; only very limited educational opportunities for women beyond the compulsory, elementary-school level were encouraged by government officials. The Civil Code of 1898 enshrined patriarchy and patrilinealism as the norm for all Japanese families and subordinated women to men in a variety of ways. Only men were legally recognized persons; women were classified in the same category as the 'deformed and mentally incompetent' and needed their father's or husband's consent before entering into a legal contract. A husband was free to dispose of his wife's property as he wished; only a wife's adultery constituted immediate grounds for divorce; in the event of divorce, the husband or his parents took custody of the children.

Official exhortation and legislation did not lead immediately to the 'samuraization' of all Japanese families, of course, but over time—largely as the result of the exposure of successive generations of young Japanese to school lessons in which the divergent role models of male and female subjects of the emperor were recurrent themes—the new norm took hold. Although Japanese feminists and other domestic critics of the *status quo ante* welcomed the bestowal of full political, social, and economic equality between men and women in occupied Japan's American-inspired constitution and civil code,[6] most adult Japanese were bemused by the sudden introduction of a radically new, egalitarian ideology of gender and remained tied, both by habit and the necessities of survival in difficult times, to the ethos they had imbibed as children.

In the circumstances prevailing in the immediate postwar years, no one proved more tied than government officials, corporate managers, and the male employees of larger enterprises.

While the active participation of women in politics was accepted, or at least tolerated, during the 1950s, their full participation in the non-agricultural, non-familial enterprise labor force met with no little resistance. Jobs were scarce, and priority had to be given to heads of households, that is, in most cases to men. Their wives could do in-home piecework (*naishoku*), if essential to the family's survival, until their unmarried daughters were old enough to contribute to household income through employment.

What might have been only a temporary adjustment to hard times was given impetus by the economic 'miracle' and the particular terms by which the management of large enterprises reasserted authority over workers and co-operative 'second unions'. Not only did the number of good, reasonably secure, and well-paying jobs for young men increase, making it possible for ever more young women to see marriage to one of them as a gateway to professional domesticity. In addition, the demands of most employers that their regular, full-time male employees work long hours and devote themselves wholeheartedly to the enterprise in order to secure advancement also virtually required that those employees have full-time wives at home, to take responsibility for keeping them fed, bathed, cleanly clothed, and off to work on time each morning, not to mention caring for any pre-school or school-age children while they, the source of the earnings that sustained the family unit, were away at the company or factory. These tasks, and the labor-intensity of housework and shopping for daily necessities at the time, kept the wife busy throughout the day and, often, well into the night. Not unimportantly, male employees in larger firms, and their unions, generally supported management's efforts to relegate women to the margins of employment as temporary workers on the assembly line or in clerical work, so as to protect the salaries, bonuses, and benefits they enjoyed as full members of the enterprise.

One consequence of these factors, at least until recently, was a pronounced M-curve in the employment pattern of Japanese women: that is, rising participation in the labor force for women from the age of about 15 until the mid-twenties; a steep decline thereafter as most women married and had children; a second, though less pronounced rise in their participation in the labor force from the age of 35 or so to about 45, when their children were (almost) grown up; and another decline thereafter. Whereas men entered the labor force and in most cases remained in it until retirement, the participation of women was responsive to life-cycle events.

Another consequence was a somewhat unusual—or unusually prolonged—pattern of motivation for female participation in higher education. In most if not all Western countries since the mid- to late 1960s, the more education a woman has had the more likely she has been to be employed, and an increasing share of young women have given preparation for a career in work as their primary purpose in enrolling in college or university. Not so in Japan. Since the late 1970s virtually all youngsters, both girls and boys, have continued to upper secondary school/high school after completing the compulsory nine years of elementary and lower secondary education mandated during the Occupation era, and since the early 1980s over one-third of both female and male upper secondary school graduates have continued to higher, or tertiary, education. But a Japanese woman with a college or university degree has been *less* likely than a woman who completed secondary education only to enter the labor force, and the duration of her participation in it, if participate she does, has been shorter than that of her counterpart with lesser educational qualifications. In other words, higher education for Japanese women appears to have functioned largely as a qualification for good, economically secure marriages to male university graduates who, by virtue of their university degrees, were able to secure posts in large corporations or government ministries. This has been reflected in the type of higher educational institution most of these women have entered—the two-year junior college (*tanki daigaku*) rather than the four-year university—and the subjects (home economics, child psychology, or literature rather than, say, law or international relations) most of them have studied.

Recently, there have been signs of change in both patterns, and the reasons for these changes provide insight into some of the major concerns of Japanese women today. The M-curve has begun to flatten, as more and more women in their twenties have prolonged their stay in the labor force and others have reduced the span of years between their retirement at marriage and re-entry after childbearing. There has also been an increase, albeit rather modest to date, in the proportion of women attending four-year universities rather than junior colleges, studying hitherto 'unfeminine' subjects and attempting—like a significant number of their Western counterparts and with much the same constant juggling of obligations—to have both a family and a career. At the risk of oversimplifying multifaceted and still unfolding trends, one can divide their probable causes into two broad categories: those which are pulling women away from a home-bound existence and those which are pushing them away from it.

The former are better documented but no more important than the latter, and consist largely of greater opportunities for the extra-domestic employment of women in the form of part-time jobs (known as *paato*), which have proliferated in Japan since the first oil crisis of 1973, and the limited opening of career-track managerial positions for women in some enterprises since the passage of an Equal Employment Opportunity Law in 1985.[7] Both reflect the rapid expansion of the tertiary sector of the economy since the mid-1970s and managerial concern with the growing scarcity (and higher cost) of young male recruits for both industry and commerce. In effect, women came to be seen as an under-utilized resource, and personnel practices were adjusted to remedy the situation. In factories, where labor shortages were most keenly felt, pressures on young women with full-time jobs on the assembly line to retire at marriage abated somewhat. Part-time jobs were created in great number in factories, offices, and retail establishments and were presented as particularly suitable for married women, because they would not be expected to work overtime and could leave for home at a predetermined hour every day to prepare dinner for their families. Provided women with suitable university degrees were willing to accept the same conditions as men, including frequent changes of job location, they became eligible for consideration as regular managerial personnel. Failing that, fixed-term but fairly well-paid posts as 'specialists' in such fields as product design, marketing, or public relations might be arranged, or women could be employed as local or office managers at lower salaries than regular managerial personnel.

These attractions from employers coincided with a variety of calculations and aspirations of a personal nature—the pushes I referred to above—which have induced ever greater numbers of women to seek to remain in or re-enter employment. For married women in their early thirties, a key factor appears to have been the growing financial cost of raising a family, and in this sense their return to paid work outside the home—almost always on a part-time basis—can be seen as an extension of mothering. While the rate of increase in the real incomes of Japanese men slowed during the 1980s, the costs of housing and education accelerated. In those circumstances, the second income brought in by wives (even if, on average, only about 20 per cent of total household income[8]) helped to pay for the mortgage on a family-sized house or condominium, the fees charged for school meals, excursions, and other extras (some 180,000 yen annually per pupil in a state elementary school and some 220,000 yen annually for a pupil in a state lower secondary school) for children between the ages of 6 and 14, or the even greater cost of high-school, college, and university education for older children.[9]

For single women in their twenties and, increasingly, in their thirties, a concern with self may well have been of primary importance. While not necessarily rejecting marriage or motherhood, they sought to postpone both while they made the most of the opportunities available to them as young adults—to put their training and talents to use in work, to enjoy the nightlife of the cities they inhabited, and to explore the world on holiday. Underlying their quest for personal fulfillment was a fairly shrewd estimation of the role of caring for others—husband, children, up to four aged parents (his and hers)—that lay ahead for them, and the paid and unpaid work for the benefit of others they would eventually have to perform. That, too, was likely to prove gratifying, at least in part, but it would also restrict them for long periods to a rather isolated existence in a high-rise apartment or house in a bedroom suburb, virtually excluded from the after-hours social life of their husbands and able to look forward only to an occasional weekend trip to a family-oriented theme park. With housework much simplified by labor-saving appliances and a multitude of convenience foods available at the local supermarket, what would they do all day once the children were in school?

The onslaught of economic recession in 1991 revealed another facet of employers' interest in women as an under-utilized resource: they were also an expendable resource and, as such, the first to be dismissed or ignored when an enterprise needed to cut its costs. Many part-time female employees lost their jobs as the recession deepened, and the ratio of job openings per female university graduate fell from 1.98 in the spring of 1991 to 0.87 in 1994. That the equivalent decline for male university graduates was from 3.14 to 1.81 indicates the fragility of the position in the upper end of the labor market that women had achieved. Even so, it would be unwise to conclude that women will retreat meekly and mutely into a purely domestic role. Not only will many of them of varying ages continue to want employment, but also employers will need them as the economy recovers and (not unimportantly) as fewer and fewer young job-seekers of either sex come of age in the years ahead.

The steadily falling lifetime birthrate of Japanese women, from 4.45 children in 1947 to 1.53 in 1991, is largely the product of decisions that women have taken about how best to maximize the life chances of their offspring in view of prevailing economic and social realities. The average age at marriage for women has not risen from 23 in the 1950s to over 26 today by accident, nor has the doubling of the percentages of 'never married' women aged 25–9 and 30–4 since the 1970s, from 18.1 per cent to 40.2 per cent and from 7.2 per cent to 13.9 per cent, respectively. People, most of them women, have been exercising an important degree of choice, and it is to them—especially to successive generations of mothers and daughters, to the modest new freedoms bestowed by the one and the slightly greater than anticipated liberties taken by the other—that we must look for a full explanation of these trends.

The Social-Management Strategies of the State

Other than eliminating the War and Navy Ministries and assigning the broad range of responsibilities once concentrated in the Home Ministry to other ministries and agencies, the Occupation authorities did little to restructure Japan's bureaucracy,[10] and it has continued to function as a major force in national life. Recruitment to its ranks is by examination at entry level, followed by selection interviews. Those university graduates who pass the highly competitive class I examination for policy-making posts and secure offers of appointment from a ministry or agency of the central government will remain with the ministry or agency whose offer they accept throughout their professional careers, except perhaps for brief periods of study abroad or secondment to another organization, and will rise gradually up its hierarchy of posts. Most will end their careers as officials of middle rank; only a few members of each entering cohort will eventually, in their early fifties, be assigned to top executive positions. After retirement in their mid-fifties, most class I officials will 'descend from heaven' (*amakudaru*) and take up a second career, often related in some way to their official career, in private industry, research institutes, or politics.[11]

Class I officials serving in central government posts in Tokyo number about 18,000 at any time. They form the undisputed élite of a relatively small national, prefectural, and local civil service that collectively (including teachers and postal-service workers as well as filing clerks and maintenance personnel) employs about 3.7 per cent of the total population. On the whole, the general public has admired civil servants, and the higher their rank the greater has been the public's admiration. Although ordinary Japanese could and did grumble about the red tape they encountered whenever they had dealings with officialdom, they tended to regard bureaucrats as honest—certainly more honest than most politicians—and dedicated to the best interests of the nation. That élite, class I officials had achieved their positions by merit as demonstrated by their success in gaining admission to prestigious universities and passing competitive examinations counted for a lot in a society where equality of opportunity (even if primarily for men) was thought to prevail. I will deal later with the issue of growing doubts about this equality, but first let me provide an example of this sector of the bureaucracy in action.

As noted earlier, the implications of a falling birthrate and a 'greying' population have sent shockwaves through the Japanese system. While some members of the political and economic establishment merely exhorted women to come to the nation's rescue by having more babies and began, in the 1980s, to denigrate the wanton selfishness of those younger women who appeared to have cast their reproductive duty aside in favor of trendy clothes, disco-dancing, and foreign travel, bureaucrats in a variety of central ministries began to study the demographic problem in all its complexity and to devise measures to deal with it. Rather than scapegoating women, they accepted the existence of obstacles to the nurturing and caring roles performed chiefly by women and, by means of research at home and abroad, as well as extensive discussions with academic experts and other advisers, considered how at least some of those obstacles might be removed. The proposals that emerged from this prolonged and wide-ranging inquiry in the early 1990s focused on housing, working conditions, and education, as well as on some restructuring of social-welfare provisions.

In 1991 a single-family dwelling with 128 meters of floor space in or near Tokyo cost 68 million yen, more than eight times the average household income in the metropolitan area, owing largely to massive increases in land prices. All but the very wealthiest among would-be home purchasers had to travel at least 60 kilometers away from the capital and incur a daily commuting time of roughly two hours each way to find properties they could afford to pay for. At the same time, the housing markets in Tokyo, Osaka, and some other large cities were glutted with small condominium apartments built by private firms, which were deemed suitable only for newly married couples, and with public housing units constructed prior to 1965 which, at about 40 square meters each in size, were suitable only for single persons. The latter were occupied increasingly by the elderly, and in some of the neighborhoods close to central business districts in which these units were located, the night-time population consisted primarily of those over the age of 60. It was essential for the government to make affordable, family-sized housing more widely available in or near major cities, chiefly by inducing lower land prices, encouraging the development of new housing sites (e.g. on landfill and on land previously devoted to farming or car parks) and by reconstructing existing public housing blocks on a larger per unit scale. A goal of '5 times in 5 years'—that is, of bringing the cost of housing in metropolitan areas down to five times average annual income, approximately the level prevailing in the rest of the country, by 1997—featured prominently in a new economic plan submitted to the then prime minister Miyazawa Kiichi in June of 1992.

Also included in that plan was the recommendation that average annual working hours be reduced from over 2,000 to 1,800 within the same five-year period. This could well require revising legislation to establish a basic forty-hour work week, down from forty-eight hours, and to raise the minimum legal pay rate for overtime as a means of encouraging the reduction of overtime work from an average of 450 to 360 hours per year. While no little foreign pressure lay behind this particular recommendation, the plan itself stressed the need to improve the quality of life of the people, by securing more time for their rest and leisure.

In a separate document, the Ministry of Education announced that, as of 1993, all students in public junior and senior high schools, boys as well as girls, would be required to take instruction in home economics. This may seem at first glance a decidedly less momentous initiative than the two described above, but its significance should not be underestimated. For a brief period in the late 1940s and early 1950s, there had been such a requirement for junior high-school students, instituted at the behest of the Occupation as part of its campaign to democratize Japanese society—even though the requirement was not at all in keeping with actual American practice at the time or for some years thereafter, as women of my generation will remember. This was amended in the late 1950s to establish separate homemaking courses for girls and industrial arts courses for boys—precisely the division that existed in the junior high school I attended—and in the 1960s, just as many schools in the United States and other Western countries were eliminating such gender-specific courses from the curriculum, home economics also became a required subject for girls, and only girls, in Japanese senior high schools.

Reflecting the then widespread belief that 'men work and women take care of the home', the rationale for these required courses became increasingly tenuous as more and more married women, roughly 65 per cent of them by the late 1980s, were out of the home at work of some sort and as public opinion surveys revealed that growing numbers of Japanese, some men as well as many women, regarded the conventional division of society into separate male and female spheres as irrational. In this context, the new home economics requirement represents a first step in redefining gender roles at the level where such redefinition is likely to have the greatest impact—among the young. It still remains to be seen whether other steps, such as the elimination of gender stereotyping from many textbooks and of the apparent discrimination against women in the administration of many schools, are also taken.

In none of these initiatives was the bearing of the new proposals on the resolution of Japan's demographic problem emphasized, but it is not difficult to see the connections. Indeed, they figure prominently in earlier reports issued by many of the same official bodies. Cheaper housing of a size adequate for family life in metropolitan areas would make it less necessary for mothers of young children in those areas to work outside the home merely to help pay for a mortgage and might encourage some of them to have an 'extra' baby. Shorter working hours would enable both men and women to devote more time and energy to their families, including to elderly parents. That young men (eventually) would understand at least the rudiments of cooking, cleaning, and child care might make them more attractive as husbands for career-minded women, and if more women married at a younger age the lifetime fertility rate of women might rise back to 2.1, insuring population replacement. To encourage even further these hoped-for developments, which would reduce the looming financial burden on the state of an aging society and the 'sapping of economic and social vitality' which that aging is thought to entail,[12] maternity benefits and aid to needy families with two or more young children would be increased, and more recreational and other day-care facilities for the elderly would be opened in local schools and other public buildings to ease the strain on adults in employment of accommodating aged parents within the family home. Cutbacks in other areas of health and welfare provision might be necessary to permit these initiatives without a marked increase in overall health and welfare costs.

It is in the indirection of contemporary bureaucratic efforts to manage Japanese society—attempts to provide inducements rather than compulsion to officially desired behavior—that the greatest contrast with the past can be detected. Macro- rather than micro-management strategies now prevail. But management still remains the bureaucracy's goal, as it has been since the Meiji era. Whether it can continue to manage successfully at a time when the problems facing Japan are, or appear to be, so much more complicated than ever before is a question which cannot be answered one way or the other at present. What is clear is that the outcome will depend in large part on continued acceptance by the Japanese people of a relatively high degree of bureaucratic intervention in their lives, and it is to the likelihood of that acceptance I now turn.

That most Japanese have accepted such bureaucratic intervention throughout most of the half-century since the end of the Second World War is not a reflection of some innate propensity within the culture. Bureaucrats have had to earn the people's respect, individually and collectively, by their achievements, and there is evidence to suggest that at both levels this may prove more problematic in future.

As has been noted in passing, the Japanese people believe in equality of opportunity. Not only is this principle enshrined in their constitution and widely celebrated as a major achievement of postwar Japan, it also has appeared to operate in practice, barring a tolerable degree of imperfection, in the decades following the end of the Second World War. The major agency through which it operated was education. According to the accepted view, every postwar child has enjoyed equal access to basic schooling, and those who have qualified for more than the basic level and for the better paid and/or more influential positions in society which additional educational credentials have brought within their reach have done so on their merits. Bright, diligently studious boys from poor families living deep in the mountainous interior of the country have been at no serious disadvantage in competition for preferment with their urban counterparts and, thanks to the steadily increasing disposable incomes of all families, girls too have been able to compete in the educational arena to a hitherto unprecedented extent. Those who have lost out in the competition have had only or primarily themselves to blame. Those who have triumphed have earned the positions they occupy and the monetary and non-monetary rewards they enjoy.

In the early postwar decades, public faith in the justice and fairness of educational selection was unsettled only very occasionally as news broke of, say, the sale of entrance examination papers for a particular high school by a corrupt member of staff or a father's attempt to bribe his son's way into medical or dental school. This was seen as illicit tampering with a fundamentally sound mechanism for allocating social functions and rewards. More recently, however, facets of the educational system itself have become controversial, and among those facets is access to higher education.

The assumption of a level playing field for children did not entail the elimination of élitism or hierarchy from the upper reaches of the educational structure. In Japan, as in many other countries, it was accepted that only a minority of young persons would qualify for a necessarily limited number of places in universities. That some universities were considered better than others, largely in terms of the career opportunities graduation from them made possible, was also accepted. What mattered was that applicants to university qualified for admission as individuals and that the best-qualified applicants gained admission to the best universities. Neither of these conditions seems as plausible as it used to be. That graduates of the University of Tokyo, the top-ranked university in Japan, are reported to earn twice the average annual income does not bother most people: the winners of the game are entitled to that. What rankles are the allegations, widely reported in the media in recent years, that the annual incomes of the *parents* of University of Tokyo students are 50 per cent higher than the national average and that roughly one-third of all successful applicants to that university attended just fifteen senior high schools, most of them located in or near major metropolitan areas, of the more than 5,000 such schools in the nation.

That variables such as family socioeconomic status and place of residence may have been impinging to a marked degree on educational selection and that the existing occupants of élite status seem to have enjoyed an advantage in transmitting their status to at least some of their children are topics that Japanese sociologists have been writing about for at least twenty years, but relatively few members of the public were aware of the analyses which purported to show that the pace of intergenerational social mobility was slackening, and even among those who were aware, few accepted that these findings could possibly apply to themselves and to their children. As is often the case, it took a specific example—in this instance, that of the University of Tokyo—presented with the stark simplicity that is associated throughout the developed world with media hype, to attract widespread attention and engender misgivings among large numbers of people about one of the central tenets of Japanese belief. Could it be that the destruction of real estate and other assets which had occurred during the final months of the Second World War, intensified by many of the reforms of the subsequent Occupation, had served merely to level Japanese society to a transient state of equality and that the old, supposedly eradicated advantages of birth had been gaining strength ever since?

Although class I bureaucrats are not the only persons to have risen by means of success in all stages of educational selection to élite positions in society, they are among the most visible targets of public uneasiness, by virtue of the close association the public makes between the bureaucracy and the University of Tokyo. It was to provide well-qualified officials and technicians for the state that the university, first created in 1877, was expanded in the late 1880s and early 1890s, and for the entire period until 1945 most bureaucrats in the service of the central government were graduates of its faculty of law. The connection weakened gradually thereafter, but even in the 1980s, graduates of that faculty and some other faculties within the university formed the largest group among candidates passing the class I examinations and securing offers of appointment. That fully 85 per cent of the new intake to the Ministry of Finance in 1985 were Tokyo University graduates is an extreme example of the continued operation of this link, but even in ministries which cast a somewhat broader recruitment net, considerable numbers of graduates of this one institution are to be found.

No one questions the basic abilities of these graduates. It is whether their abilities have been fairly nurtured and tested, hence qualifying them to act on behalf of the nation as a whole and to be heeded when they attempt to do so, that is increasingly at issue. To the extent that they are perceived as coming disproportionately from already privileged backgrounds—from the upper middle classes of metropolitan Japan—their neutrality is compromised and their stature as defenders of the broader public interest reduced, especially among the many Japanese who do not live in Greater Tokyo and a few other metropolitan areas.

The problems confronting bureaucrats as individuals have been compounded by the sudden ending of the long ascendancy of the Liberal Democratic Party in 1993 and by the less dramatic but no less important workings of generational change. Unshielded, at least for the time being, by a single political party with majority status within the Diet, the bureaucracy as a whole stands more exposed to public scrutiny than at any time since 1955, and mistakes in policy or biases in favor of decidedly 'special' interests by any of its constituent parts are considerably more difficult to disguise or deflect. Nor are those Japanese who were born after about 1960 and for whom the privations of the war years and early postwar era hold no personal meaning as likely as their parents or grandparents were to be satisfied with plans and policies which promise gradual solutions to the problems they face in their daily lives, even though gradual solutions may now be all that any honest government anywhere in the world can offer its citizens. Japanese men and women in their mid-thirties or younger, who have grown up in a wealthy country, expect to be able to enjoy more of the amenities of life, on a par with their counterparts in many Western countries whose disposable incomes are not even as high as theirs, and they will not be pleased or easily placated if any ministry or agency seeks to impede them.

It is always tempting to see the present as a turning-point, and to assign to unfolding events or trends a significance they may not in the end deserve, but I cannot help feeling that the temptation is justified so far as contemporary Japanese society is concerned. Not only have a number of complicated problems surfaced in recent years; those problems and their possible remedies are also being considered on an unprecedented scale, by ordinary citizens as well as by bureaucrats and other members of Japan's élite. It will be interesting to see what solutions emerge in the years ahead, and to what extent changes in the relationship between the people and the state also occur. I figure that the people have their best chance ever, far exceeding the leverage they enjoyed during the 1920s or during the postwar Occupation, to influence the outcome, and I attribute much of the continuing disarray in Japanese politics since the ending of LDP ascendancy in 1993 to recognition of this fact among many of the nation's politicians.

Notes

Chapter 1 (pages 8–21)

1. Tr. R. M. Spaulding, 'The Intent of the Charter Oath', in R. K. Beardsley, ed., *Studies in Japanese History and Politics* (Center for Japanese Studies Occasional Papers, 10; Univ. of Mich. Press, 1967), 3–36.
2. Preamble to the Fundamental Code of Education, 1876, quoted in H. Passin, *Society and Education in Japan* (Kodansha International Ltd., 1982), 211.
3. J. F. Lowder, quoted in W. E. Griffis, *The Mikado's Empire* (Harper & Brothers, 1876), 292.
4. See J. R. Strayer, 'The Tokugawa Period and Japanese Feudalism', in J. W. Hall and M. B. Jansen, eds., *Studies in the Institutional History of Early Modern Japan* (Princeton UP, 1968), 3–14.
5. T. C. Smith, ' "Merit" as Ideology in the Tokugawa Period', in R. P. Dore, ed., *Aspects of Social Change in Modern Japan* (Princeton UP, 1967), repr. in T. C. Smith, *Native Sources of Japanese Industrialization, 1750–1920* (Univ. of Calif. Press, 1988), 169.
6. G. B. Sansom, *The Western World and Japan* (Alfred A. Knopf, 1958), 254.

Chapter 2 (pages 22–34)

1. Kaneko Kentarō, quoted in K. B. Pyle, 'The Technology of Japanese Nationalism: The Local Improvement Movement 1900–1918', *Journal of Asian Studies*, 33: 1 (1973), 54. Emphasis added.
2. Ibid.
3. The official English tr., quoted in G. B. Sansom, *The Western World and Japan* (Alfred A. Knopf, 1958), 464.
4. Quoted in K. B. Pyle, 'Meiji Conservatism', in M. B. Jansen, ed., *The Cambridge History of Japan* (Cambridge UP, 1989), 715.
5. Quoted in Kimmochi Saionji, 'National Education in the Meiji Era', in Shigenobu Okuma, *Fifty Years of New Japan*, ii (Smith, Elder, & Co., 1909), 167.

Chapter 3 (pages 35–53)

1. Quoted in W. L. Neumann, *America Encounters Japan: From Perry to MacArthur* (The Johns Hopkins Press, 1963), 47.
2. See S. B. Hanley and K. Yamamura, *Economic and Demographic Change in Preindustrial Japan, 1600–1868* (Princeton UP, 1977), esp. 226–66; also, T. C. Smith, with R. Y. Eng and R. T. Lundy, *Nakahara: Family Farming and Population in a Japanese Village, 1717–1830* (Stanford UP, 1977).
3. T. C. Smith, *Political Change and Industrial Development in Japan: Government Enterprise, 1868–1880* (Stanford UP, 1955), 97.
4. Ibid. 96–7.
5. K. Yamamura, *A Study of Samurai Income and Entrepreneurship* (Harvard UP, 1974), 178.

Chapter 4 (pages 54–75)

1. See A. Gordon, *Labor and Imperial Democracy in Prewar Japan* (Univ. of Calif. Press, 1991), 26–62.
2. Since 1911 a city (*shi*) had been defined as an urban district with a population of at least 30,000. Not until 1943, when the minimum level of population was increased to 50,000, was it stipulated that at least 60% of all households should be engaged in commerce or industry and that at least 60% of all buildings should be contiguous. Even in 1925, however, some 55% of all cities had populations in excess of 50,000, and a relatively high degree of non-agricultural activity and density of buildings within them can be assumed.
3. E. S. Crawcour, 'Industrialization and Technological Change, 1885–1920', in P. Duus, ed., *The Cambridge History of Japan*, vi (Cambridge UP, 1988), 406.
4. M. Yasuzawa, 'Changes in Lifestyle in Japan: Patterns and Structure of Modern Consumption', in H. Baudet and H. van der Meulen, eds., *Consumer Behavior and Economic Growth in the Modern Economy* (Croom Helm, 1983), 198. See also Gordon, *Labor and Imperial Democracy*, 19.
5. Quoted in A. Waswo, 'In Search of Equity: Japanese Tenant Unions in the 1920s', in T. Najita and J. V. Koschmann, eds., *Conflict in Modern Japanese History: The Neglected Tradition* (Princeton UP, 1982), 394.
6. Quoted in T. C. Smith, 'The Right to Benevolence: Dignity and Japanese Workers, 1890–1920', *Comparative Studies in Society and History*, 26: 4 (1984), repr. in T. C. Smith, *Native Sources of Japanese Industrialization, 1750–1920* (Univ. of Calif. Press, 1988), 259.

7. Quoted in Hayashi Yūichi and Yasuda Hiroshi, 'Shakai udnō no shosō', in Rekishigaku Kenkyūkai, Nihonshi Kenkyūkai, eds., *Kōza Nihon rekishi*, ix. (Tōkyō Daigaku Shuppankai, 1985), 199.
8. Quoted in Waswo, 'In Search of Equity', 390.
9. Quoted in Takahashi Iichirō and Shirakawa Kiyoshi, eds., *Nōchi kaikaku to jinushi sei* (Ochanomizu Shobō, 1955), 97.

Chapter 5 (pages 76–89)

1. See Taichirō Mitani, 'The Establishment of Party Cabinets, 1898–1932', in P. Duus, ed., *The Cambridge History of Japan*, vi (Cambridge UP, 1988), 55–96.
2. G. J. Kasza, *The State and the Mass Media in Japan, 1918–1945* (Univ. of Calif. Press, 1988), 283.
3. A complete tr. of the Meiji Constitution appears in G. M. Beckmann, *The Making of the Meiji Constitution: The Oligarchs and the Constitutional Development of Japan, 1868–1891* (Greenwood Press, 1975), 150–6, and in G. Itasaka, ed., *The Kodansha Encyclopedia of Japan*, ii (Kodansha International/USA Ltd., 1983), 7–9.
4. The full text appears in H. Lory, *Japan's Military Masters: The Army in Japanese Life* (Greenwood Press, 1973), 239–45.

Chapter 6 (pages 90–103)

1. B. W. F. Powell, 'Some Colonies in Spirit: Japanese Theatre and Literature in the Modern Period', paper presented to the Asian Studies Seminar, St Antony's College, Oxford, 1 May 1984.
2. 'Towarete iru no wa Nippon no kokka imeeji', *Chūō Kōron* (Oct. 1982), 110.
3. 'Tradition and Politics in Contemporary Japan', draft seminar paper, 1973, p. 9; later publ. as 'Tradition and Politics in Studies of Contemporary Japan', *World Politics*, 26: 3 (1974), 400–27, but this Fig. 2 does not appear there.
4. Quoted in K. B. Pyle, *The New Generation in Meiji Japan: Problems of Cultural Identity 1885–1895* (Stanford UP, 1969), 70.
5. Quoted in ibid. 36.
6. Quoted in ibid. 25.
7. Quoted in ibid. 56.
8. Quoted in ibid. 92.
9. Quoted in ibid. 178, 181.
10. Key portions of Tanizaki's essay are tr. by E. G. Seidensticker in *Japan Quarterly*, 1: 1 (1954), 46–52. For a complete tr., by T. J.

Harper and E. G. Seidensticker, see J. Tanizaki, *In Praise of Shadows* (Jonathan Cape, 1991).
11. *Nihonjin no nō: nō no hataraki to tōzai no bunka* (Taishūkan Shoten, 1978); tr. Y. Oiwa as *The Japanese Brain: Uniqueness and Universality* (The Taishukan Publishing Co., 1985).
12. 'The Future of Japanese Nationality: An Essay in Contemporary History', *Journal of Japanese Studies*, 8: 2 (1982), 230–1.
13. Ibid. 240.
14. Quoted in ibid. 231–2.

Chapter 7 (pages 104–26)

1. C. Johnson, 'MITI and Japanese International Economic Policy', in R. A. Scalapino, ed., *The Foreign Policy of Modern Japan* (Univ. of Calif. Press, 1977), 276.
2. H. Patrick and H. Rosovsky, 'Japan's Economic Performance: An Overview', in H. Patrick and H. Rosovsky, eds., *Asia's New Giant: How the Japanese Economy Works* (The Brookings Institution, 1976), 45.
3. Quoted in A. Gordon, *The Evolution of Labor Relations in Japan: Heavy Industry, 1853–1955* (Harvard UP, 1988), 311.
4. A. Gordon, 'Contests for the Workplace', in A. Gordon, ed., *Postwar Japan as History* (Univ. of Calif. Press, 1993), 379.
5. These trios of consumer desires are a playful rendering, much celebrated in the mass media, of the three imperial regalia: mirror, sword, and jewel. Other versions of the 'three electric treasures' include electric fans, vacuum cleaners, or rice cookers. In the early 1970s, attention switched from the by then fairly ordinary 'three Cs' to the 'three Js'—*jūeru, jetto*, and *jūtaku* (jewels, overseas vacations, and a house)—or to the 'three V's'—video, *vacances*, and villa in the mountains or some other resort area.
6. As defined by a doctor at the National Institute of Public Health, *karōshi* is 'a condition in which a worker's normal daily rhythms are disrupted by continuing unsound work patterns, resulting in a buildup of fatigue. The exhaustion induced by chronic overwork aggravates preexistent health problems, such as high blood pressure and hardening of the arteries, and causes a life-threatening crisis'. See H. Kawahito, 'Death and the Corporate Warrior', *Japan Quarterly*, 38: 2 (1991), 149–57.
7. Quoted in J. Unger, 'Pollution Proves Killer in Japanese Cities', *Asian Reports* (6 Mar. 1972), 2.
8. 'Fisheries and Industrial Pollution', *Japan Quarterly*, 20: 4 (1973), 375.

Chapter 8 (pages 127–63)

1. Bernard Eccleston, *State and Society in Post-War Japan* (Polity Press, 1989), 60, 178–9, 197.
2. G. B. Sansom, *Japan: A Short Cultural History*, revised edn. (Appleton-Century-Crofts, Inc., 1962), 465.
3. See G. L. Curtis, *The Japanese Way of Politics* (Columbia UP, 1988), 49–61; also M. W. Donnelly, 'Setting the Price of Rice: A Study in Political Decisionmaking', in T. J. Pempel, ed., *Policymaking in Contemporary Japan* (Cornell UP, 1977), 143–200.
4. International Research Group, Ministry of Finance, *Public Finance and Tax System in Japan* (Foundation for Advanced Information and Research (FAIR), 1992), 186.
5. See E. F. Vogel, *Japan's New Middle Class*, 2nd edn. (Univ. of Calif. Press, 1971).
6. See S. J. Pharr, 'The Politics of Women's Rights', in R. E. Ward and Y. Sakamoto, eds., *Democratizing Japan: The Allied Occupation* (Univ. of Hawaii Press, 1987), 221–52.
7. See A. Lam, 'Equal Employment Opportunities for Japanese Women: Changing Company Practice', in J. Hunter, ed., *Japanese Women Working* (Routledge, 1993), 197–223.
8. Eccleston, *State and Society*, 192.
9. H. Cortazzi, *Modern Japan: A Concise Survey* (Macmillan, 1993), 172–3, 178. For the parents of two children, one in a state elementary school and one in a state lower secondary school, the annual bill for these fees would amount to some 400,000 yen (the equivalent of roughly £2,600 or $4,000 at the exchange rates prevailing in the early 1990s). The annual cost of private schooling is considerably higher.
10. See T. J. Pempel, 'The Tar Baby Target: "Reform" of the Japanese Bureaucracy', in Ward and Sakamoto, eds., *Democratizing Japan*, 157–87.
11. See A. Kubota, *Higher Civil Servants in Postwar Japan: Their Social Origins, Educational Backgrounds, and Career Patterns* (Princeton UP, 1969); also Albrecht Rothacher, *The Japanese Power Elite* (St Martin's Press, 1993), 123–79.
12. 'Advisory panel report points to dangers of falling birthrate', *News & Views from Japan*, 345 (The Information Centre of the Mission of Japan to the European Community, 2 July 1990), 5.

Select Bibliography

General

Most general surveys of modern Japanese history emphasize politics, foreign policy, and war. Of those which give more than passing attention to society and social change, the best is K. B. Pyle, *The Making of Modern Japan* (D. C. Heath and Co., 1978), which will soon be available in a new edition. Also useful are P. Duus, *The Rise of Modern Japan* (Houghton Mifflin Co., 1976) and J. E. Hunter, *The Emergence of Modern Japan* (Longman, 1989).

The multi-volume *Kodansha Encyclopedia of Japan* (Kodansha, 1983) contains over 10,000 entries, including many on society and culture in the modern era. Most entries provide bibliographic references, and an index volume makes the encyclopedia easy to use. See J. W. Dower, *Japanese History and Culture from Ancient to Modern Times: Seven Basic Bibliographies* (Univ. of Manchester Press, 1985) for references to books and articles published up through the mid-1980s on early modern and modern Japan (Bibliography 2: 1600–1945).

A number of interpretations of modern Japanese society and culture exist, the most well-known being C. Nakane, *Japanese Society* (Univ. of Calif. Press, 1970) and T. Doi, *The Anatomy of Dependence* (Kodansha International Ltd., 1973). Both are certainly worth reading, but it should be remembered that neither provides more than a partial explanation of a multifaceted and constantly changing reality. Of this genre, I much prefer the more nuanced R. J. Smith, *Japanese Society: Tradition, Self and the Social Order* (Cambridge UP, 1983) and J. Hendry, *Understanding Japanese Society* (Croom Helm, 1987; 2nd edn. Routledge, 1995).

On the Meiji Restoration

For a brief and lucid discussion of how the Tokugawa shogunate was overthrown and a new regime established, see M. B. Jansen, 'The Meiji Restoration', in M. B. Jansen, ed., *The Cambridge History of Japan*, V (Cambridge UP, 1989), 308–66. For insight into the role of commoners in these events, see G. M. Wilson, *Patriots and Redeemers in Japan: Motives in the Meiji Restoration* (Univ. of Chicago Press, 1992).

The final portion of Conrad Totman, *Japan Before Perry: A Brief Synthesis* (Univ. of Calif. Press, 1982) provides a useful overview of the major institutions of the Tokugawa shogunate and of economic and social change during the Tokugawa period. For more detailed exploration of these topics and of brewing discontent among members of the warrior class, see R. P. Dore, *Education in Tokugawa Japan* (Univ. of Calif. Press, 1965); T. C. Smith, 'Pre-Modern Economic Growth: Japan and the West', *Past and Present*, 60 (1973), 127–60; ' "Merit" as Ideology in the Tokugawa Period', in R. P. Dore, ed., *Aspects of Social Change in Modern Japan* (Princeton UP, 1967), 71–90; and 'Japan's Aristocratic Revolution', *Yale Review* (1961), 370–83. The last three are repr. in T. C. Smith, *Native Sources of Japanese Industrialization* (Univ. of Calif. Press, 1988).

Creating the New Nation

Further exploration of the topics discussed in Ch. 2 should begin with two excellent articles by K. B. Pyle: 'Advantages of Followership: German Economics and Japanese Bureaucrats, 1890–1925', *Journal of Japanese Studies*, 1: 1 (1974), 127–64, and 'The Technology of Japanese Nationalism: The Local Improvement Movement 1900–1918', *Journal of Asian Studies*, 33: 1 (1973), 51–65. One should then tackle Carol Gluck's richly documented and perceptive study of the imperial institution, *Japan's Modern Myths: Ideology in the Late Meiji Period* (Princeton UP, 1985).

On education in the Meiji era, the most comprehensive source remains H. Passin, *Society and Education in Japan* (Kondansha International Ltd., 1982), but see also I. Amano, *Education and Examination in Modern Japan*, tr. W. K. Cummings and F. Cummings (Univ. of Tokyo Press, 1990); R. Rubinger, 'Education: From One Room to One System', in M. B. Jansen and G. Rozman, eds., *Japan in Transition: From Tokugawa to Meiji* (Princeton UP, 1986), 195–230; and the fascinating exploration of higher schools in D. T. Roden, *Schooldays in Imperial Japan: A Study in the Culture of a Student Elite* (Univ. of Calif. Press, 1980).

For an intriguing case study of efforts to redraw the administrative map of Japan, see N. L. Waters, *Japan's Local Pragmatists: The Transition from Bakumatsu to Meiji in the Kawasaki Region* (Harvard UP, 1983). That commoners were far from passive bystanders in the events of the Restoration era and in diverse ways resisted many of the centralizing initiatives emanating from Tokyo is revealed in W. W. Kelly, *Deference and Defiance in Nineteenth Century Japan* (Princeton UP, 1985), R. W. Bowen, *Rebellion and Democracy in Meiji Japan: A Study of Commoners in the Popular Rights Movement* (Univ. of Calif. Press, 1980), and Irokawa

Daikichi, *The Culture of the Meiji Period* (Princeton UP, 1985), tr. ed. M. B. Jansen.

Toward an Industrial Economy

For the general reader, the most useful accounts of Japan's modern economic development are E. S. Crawcour, 'Economic Change in the Nineteenth Century', in M. B. Jansen, ed., *The Cambridge History of Japan*, v (Cambridge UP, 1989), 569–617, and 'Industrialization and Technological Change, 1885–1920', in P. Duus, ed., *The Cambridge History of Japan*, vi (Cambridge UP, 1988), 385–450. Still unsurpassed as a comprehensive but not unduly technical discussion is W. W. Lockwood, *The Economic Development of Japan: Growth and Structural Change 1868–1938* (Princeton UP, 1968). See also G. C. Allen, *A Short Economic History of Modern Japan*, 4th edn. (The Macmillan Press Ltd., 1981).

On developments during the Tokugawa period which facilitated Japan's later economic transformation, see S. B. Hanley and K. Yamamura, *Economic and Demographic Change in Preindustrial Japan, 1600–1868* (Princeton UP, 1977); W. B. Hauser, *Economic Institutional Change in Tokugawa Japan: Osaka and the Kinai Cotton Trade* (Cambridge UP, 1974); T. C. Smith, *The Agrarian Origins of Modern Japan* (Stanford UP, 1959); and, by the same author, the following exceptionally finely crafted articles, all of them repr. in his *Native Sources of Japanese Industrialization, 1750–1920* (Univ. of Calif. Press, 1988): 'Farm Family By-Employments in Preindustrial Japan', *Journal of Economic History*, 29: 4 (1969), 687–715, 'Ōkura Nagatsune and the Technologists', in A. Craig and D. H. Shively, eds., *Personality in Japanese History* (Univ. of Calif. Press, 1970), and 'Peasant Time and Factory Time in Japan', *Past and Present*, 111 (May 1986), 165–97.

The role of the state in the development of economically useful infrastructure is ably explored in T. C. Smith, *Political Change and Industrial Development in Japan: Government Enterprise, 1868–1880* (Stanford UP, 1955) and D. E. Westney, *Imitation and Innovation: The Transfer of Western Organizational Patterns to Meiji Japan* (Harvard UP, 1987), especially her discussions of the police and the postal system.

On entrepreneurship and other aspects of the popular response to new opportunities in the Meiji era (except by industrial laborers and farmers, about which see below), the best available accounts are K. Yamamura, *A Study of Samurai Income and Entrepreneurship* (Harvard UP, 1974), ch. 7–9; J. Hirschmeier and T. Yui, *The Development of Japanese Business, 1600–1980*, 2nd edn. (George Allen & Unwin, 1981); M. Fruin, *Kikkoman: Company, Clan, and Community* (Harvard UP, 1983); W. D. Wray,

Mitsubishi and the N.Y.K., 1870–1914: Business Strategy in the Japanese Shipping Industry (Harvard UP, 1984); E. H. Kinmonth, *The Self-Made Man in Meiji Japanese Thought: From Samurai to Salary Man* (Univ. of Calif. Press, 1981); and B. K. Marshall, *Capitalism and Nationalism in Prewar Japan: The Ideology of the Business Elite, 1868–1941* (Stanford UP, 1967).

A welcome new addition to this literature, which broadens the inquiry into the dynamics of economic development well beyond the state and large enterprises, is T. Morris-Suzuki, *The Technological Transformation of Japan: From the Seventeenth to the Twenty-first Century* (Cambridge UP, 1994).

Protest from Below

That there are still relatively few books and articles available in English on the lives, aspirations, and actions of ordinary Japanese during the first three decades of the twentieth century is a lamentable fact, but fortunately the items that have been published, mostly in the past decade or so, are generally of high quality.

Among the most impressive studies are two by A. Gordon—*The Evolution of Labor Relations in Japan: Heavy Industry, 1853–1955* (Harvard UP, 1988) and *Labor and Imperial Democracy in Prewar Japan* (Univ. of Calif. Press, 1991)—and M. Lewis's wide-ranging examination of the Rice Riots of 1918, *Rioters and Citizens: Mass Protest in Imperial Japan* (Univ. of Calif. Press, 1990).

Also well worth reading are T. C. Smith, 'The Right to Benevolence: Dignity and Japanese Workers, 1890–1920', *Comparative Studies in Society and History*, 26: 4 (1984), 587–613, repr. in his *Native Sources of Japanese Industrialization, 1750–1920* (Univ. of Calif. Press, 1988); Sheldon Garon, *The State and Labor in Modern Japan* (Univ. of Calif. Press, 1987); A. Waswo, 'In Search of Equity: Japanese Tenant Unions in the 1920s', in T. Najita and J. V. Koschmann, eds., *Conflict in Modern Japanese History: The Neglected Tradition* (Princeton UP, 1982), 366–411, and, by the same author, 'The Transformation of Rural Society, 1900–1950', in P. Duus, ed., *The Cambridge History of Japan*, vi (Cambridge UP, 1988), 541–605.

On women in these years, see E. P. Tsurumi, *Factory Girls: Women in the Thread Mills of Meiji Japan* (Princeton UP, 1990); S. Sievers, *Flowers in Salt: The Beginnings of Feminist Consciousness in Modern Japan* (Stanford UP, 1983); R. J. Smith and E. L. Wiswell, *The Women of Suye Mura* (Univ. of Chicago Press, 1982); and part ii of G. L. Bernstein, ed., *Recreating Japanese Women, 1600–1945* (Univ. of Calif. Press, 1991) on the discourse on family, gender, and work, 1868–1945.

On other aspects of the social history and social movements of this period, the most useful publications are I. Neary, *Political Protest and Social Control in Pre-war Japan: The Origins of Buraku Liberation* (Manchester UP, 1989); M. Weiner, *The Origins of the Korean Community in Japan, 1910–1923* (Manchester UP, 1989) and H. D. Smith II, *Japan's First Student Radicals* (Harvard UP, 1972). Although some extremely interesting primary source material is translated in M. Hane, *Peasants, Rebels, and Outcastes: The Underside of Modern Japan* (Pantheon, 1982), the author places undue emphasis on the desperate poverty of the masses, implying (incorrectly, in my opinion) that this was a major cause of protest. For a more likely, albeit fictional, portrayal of the effects of poverty, see T. Nagatsuka, *The Soil*, tr. A. Waswo (Univ. of Calif. Press, 1993).

The Military in Politics

On the Meiji era, one might begin with E. H. Norman, *Soldier and Peasant in Japan: The Origins of Conscription* (Institute of Pacific Relations, 1965); D. E. Westney, 'The Military', in M. B. Jansen and G. Rozman, eds., *Japan in Transition: From Tokugawa to Meiji* (Princeton UP, 1986), 168–94; J. B. Crowley, 'From Closed Door to Empire: The Foundation of the Meiji Military Establishment', in B. Silberman and H. Harootunian, eds., *Modern Japanese Leadership* (Univ. of Arizona Press, 1966), 261–85; N. Ike, 'War and Modernization', in R. E. Ward, ed., *Political Development in Modern Japan* (Princeton UP, 1968), 189–211; and S. Lone, *Japan's First Modern War: Army and Society in the Conflict with China, 1894–95* (St Martin's Press, 1994).

Although overly sweeping in his conclusions, R. J. Smethurst provides a basically sound account of efforts by the army to mobilize the people from about 1910 onward in *A Social Basis for Prewar Japanese Militarism: The Army and the Rural Community* (Univ. of Calif. Press, 1974), and G. J. Kasza indirectly provides an excellent analysis of the evolving role of the army in influencing popular thought in *The State and the Mass Media in Japan, 1918–1945* (Univ. of Calif. Press, 1988).

For discussions of intra- and inter-service rivalry, see B. A. Shillony, *Revolt in Japan: The Young Officers and the February 26, 1936 Incident* (Princeton UP, 1973); J. B. Crowley, *Japan's Quest for Autonomy: National Security and Foreign Policy, 1930–1938* (Princeton UP, 1968); and S. Asada, 'The Japanese Navy and the United States', in D. Borg and S. Okamoto, eds., *Pearl Harbor as History: Japanese–American Relations 1931–1941* (Columbia UP, 1973), 225–59. Despite its origin as a 'know the enemy' book, first published by Viking in 1943, and its lack of methodological rigor, H. Lory, *Japan's Military Masters: The Army in Japanese Life* (Greenwood Press, 1973) remains a good source of information on the training of army officers and conscripts in the 1930s.

On the experiences of ordinary soldiers, sailors, and civilians during the Asian/Pacific War, see S. Ienaga, *The Pacific War, 1931–1945* (Random House, 1978); H. T. Cook and T. F. Cook, *Japan at War: An Oral History* (New Press, 1992); T. Morris-Suzuki, *Showa: An Inside History of Hirohito's Japan* (The Athlone Press, 1984); and T. R. H. Havens, *Valley of Darkness: The Japanese People and World War Two* (Norton, 1978; also UP of America, Inc., 1986). For a revealing examination of the portrayal of this conflict to the respective populations of Japan and the United States, see J. W. Dower, *War Without Mercy: Race and Power in the Pacific War* (Pantheon Books, 1986).

Modernization and its Discontents

In the writing of Ch. 6, I have drawn heavily on K. B. Pyle, *The New Generation in Meiji Japan: Problems of Cultural Identity, 1885–1895* (Stanford UP, 1969); by the same author, 'The Future of Japanese Nationality: An Essay in Contemporary History', *Journal of Japanese Studies*, 8: 2 (1982), 223–63; and M. Fletcher, *The Search for a New Order: Intellectuals and Fascism in Prewar Japan* (Univ. of North Carolina Press, 1982). Also of great value for understanding the interwar era are P. Duus, 'Nagai Ryūtarō: The Tactical Dilemmas of Reform', in A. Craig and D. Shively, eds., *Personality in Japanese History* (Univ. of Calif. Press, 1970), 399–424; by the same author, 'Liberal Intellectuals and Social Conflict in Taishō Japan', in T. Najita and J. V. Koschmann, eds., *Conflict in Modern Japanese History: The Neglected Tradition* (Princeton UP, 1982), 412–40; and J. Crowley, 'Intellectuals as Visionaries of the New Asian Order', in J. Morley, ed., *Dilemmas of Growth in Prewar Japan* (Princeton UP, 1971), 319–73. For a radically different assessment of *Nihonjinron* than the one I present, and with which I almost entirely disagree, see P. Dale, *The Myth of Japanese Uniqueness* (Croom Helm, 1986). See also K. Yoshino, *Cultural Nationalism in Contemporary Japan: A Sociological Enquiry* (Routledge, 1992).

The Postwar 'Economic Miracle' and its Consequences

From this point onward, readers curious to learn more about Japan are faced with an abundance of books and articles in English, most of them written by scholars in disciplines other than history. It is a good idea to look at the date of publication of any item, as a study based on fieldwork in, say, the early 1970s, is unlikely to provide an accurate account of its subject in the 1990s, even if written in the present tense.

On the sources of sustained high rates of economic growth in the 'miracle years' from the mid-1950s to the early 1970s, the most wide-ranging and persuasive source remains H. Patrick and H. Rosovsky, eds., *Asia's New Giant: How the Japanese Economy Works* (Brookings Institution, 1976). Note the present tense in the title, and the date. Also extremely valuable is C. Johnson, *MITI and the Japanese Miracle: The Growth of Industrial Policy, 1925-1975* (Stanford UP, 1982). For a historian's recent and perceptive assault on this subject, see L. E. Hein, 'Growth Versus Success: Japan's Economic Policy in Historical Perspective', in A. Gordon, ed., *Postwar Japan as History* (Univ. of Calif. Press, 1993), 99-122. For a fairly brief and interesting discussion by a Japanese scholar, see Y. Kōsai, 'The Postwar Japanese Economy, 1945-1973', in P. Duus, ed., *The Cambridge History of Japan*, vi (Cambridge UP, 1988), 494-537.

On labor relations and the much-misunderstood Japanese employment system, the most important sources are A. Gordon, *The Evolution of Labor Relations in Japan: Heavy Industry, 1853-1955* (Harvard UP, 1988), especially part four on the postwar settlement; by the same author, 'Contests for the Workplace', in A. Gordon, ed., *Postwar Japan as History* (Univ. of Calif. Press, 1993), 373-94; T. P. Rohlen, *For Harmony and Strength: Japanese White-Collar Organization in Anthropological Perspective* (Univ. of Calif. Press, 1974); Rodney Clark, *The Japanese Company* (Yale UP, 1979); R. E. Cole, *Japanese Blue Collar: The Changing Tradition* (Univ. of Calif. Press, 1971); and N. Chalmers, *Industrial Relations in Japan: The Peripheral Workforce* (Routledge, 1989). See also B. Eccleston, *State and Society in Post-War Japan* (Polity Press, 1989).

On the costs of growth, see J. W. Bennett and S. B. Levine, 'Industrialization and Social Deprivation: Welfare, Environment, and the Postindustrial Society in Japan', in H. Patrick, ed., *Japanese Industrialization and its Social Consequences* (Univ. of Calif. Press, 1976), 439-92; J. Ui, ed., *Industrial Pollution in Japan* (United Nations UP, 1992); N. Huddle and M. Reich, with N. Stiskin, *Island of Dreams: Environmental Crisis in Japan* (Autumn Press, 1974); M. McKean, *Environmental Protest and Citizen Politics in Japan* (Univ. of Calif. Press, 1981); and K. Inoguchi, 'Prosperity Without the Amenities', *Journal of Japanese Studies*, 13: 1 (1987), 125-34.

Japanese Society in the Early 1990s

As a historian, I wrote Ch. 8 with no little trepidation and insinuated rather a lot of background material into the text to ease the discomfort I experienced in dealing with an ongoing, as yet uncompleted present. The references I provide below reflect the same disciplinary caution and bias. I cite only those items that made sense to me on first reading, primarily because they linked the present with the past in some way or because I understood them immediately, without having first to master a new vocabulary or set of conceptual tools.

On farmers and farming, I would recommend R. P. Dore, *Shinohata: A Portrait of a Japanese Village* (Pantheon, 1978); R. J. Smith, *Kurusu: The Price of Progress in a Japanese Village, 1951–1975* (Stanford UP, 1978); and G. L. Bernstein, *Haruko's World: A Japanese Farm Woman and her Community* (Stanford UP, 1983), of which an updated version is forthcoming.

On women, I would recommend M. C. Brinton, *Women and the Economic Miracle: Gender and Work in Postwar Japan* (Univ. of Calif. Press, 1993); K. S. Uno, 'The Death of "Good Wife, Wise Mother"?', in A. Gordon, ed., *Postwar Japan as History* (Univ. of Calif. Press, 1993), 293–322; G. S. Roberts, *Staying on the Line: Blue-Collar Women in Contemporary Japan* (Univ. of Hawaii Press, 1994); J. Lo, *Office Ladies, Factory Women: Life and Work at a Japanese Company* (M. E. Sharpe, 1990); A. Lam, *Women and Japanese Management: Discrimination and Reform* (Routledge, 1992); J. Hendry, 'The Role of the Professional Housewife', in J. Hunter, ed., *Japanese Women Working* (Routledge, 1993), 224–41; and S. Iwao, *The Japanese Woman: Tradition, Image and Changing Reality* (The Free Press, 1993), with the caveat that the latter book deals almost exclusively with highly educated, middle-class women.

On education and educational selection, see T. P. Rohlen, *Japan's High Schools* (Univ. of Calif. Press, 1983) and by the same author, 'Is Japanese Education Becoming Less Egalitarian? Notes on High School Stratification and Reform', *Journal of Japanese Studies*, 3: 1 (1977), 37–70. For a persuasive, albeit sometimes highly technical, analysis of the slackening pace of intergenerational social mobility, see H. Ishida, *Social Mobility in Contemporary Japan* (Stanford UP, 1993; also Macmillan, 1993, repr. with corrections 1995).

Index

agriculture 39–41, 42–3, 44–5, 49–50, 136–40, 142–7
 see also farmers and rural society; food safety; food security
alternate attendance 12–13
Araki Masuo 123–4, 125
army, *see* military (to 1945)

Boshin Rescript 28–9
bureaucracy:
 and nation-building in the Meiji period 23–34, 148–9
 popular attitudes toward (since 1945) 155–6, 159–63
 responses to social unrest 56, 72, 74–5
 and the warrior class 16–17, 22
 see also economic development; Home Ministry; Ministry of Agriculture, Forestry and Fisheries (MAFF); Ministry of Education; Ministry of International Trade and Industry (MITI)

Charter Oath 8, 91
Civil Code (1898) 149

economic development
 entrepreneurship 51–3, 112, 113
 and international economic environment 35–6, 37–9, 106–7, 108–9
 popular attitudes toward 51, 52, 53, 110, 118–19, 123–4, 126
 and postwar labor relations 113–18
 state's role in 43–50, 107–8, 110–13
 in the Tokugawa period 12–13, 14–15, 39–43
 women in 42–3, 61, 117
 see also agriculture; environmental pollution; industrial labor force
education:
 cost of 153
 entrance examinations 127, 128
 and equality of opportunity 159–61, 162
 gender differences in 148, 151, 152, 157–8
 in the Meiji period 25, 28, 29–30, 33–4, 58, 93
 and popular protest 63–5
 in the Tokugawa period 16–17, 42
elderly, in contemporary Japan 132–4, 141, 157, 158, 159
emperor and imperial institution 10–11, 26–9, 33, 65, 78
employment, *see* farmers and rural society, industrial labor force; Japanese employment system; labor disputes; women
environmental pollution, 119–22, 123–4, 125–6

farmers and rural society 13–14, 15, 30–3, 49–50, 57–60, 134–47

farmers and rural society (*cont.*)
  see also land reform; tenancy disputes
First World War 61, 71, 82–4
food safety 119–20, 125, 134, 147
food security 134, 144, 147

Great Kantō Earthquake 54

Home Ministry 31, 114, 155
housing and housing problems 123, 127, 128–9, 136, 142, 153, 156–7, 158

Imperial Rescript on Education 28, 30
Imperial Rescript to Soldiers and Sailors 79–80
industrial labor force 60-3, 66–7
  see also Japanese employment system; labor disputes; women
industrialization, see economic development
itai itai disease 120, 123

Japan, Western image of 127–8
Japanese employment system 74, 113–14, 117–18, 131–2

Kozaki Hiromichi 93
Kuga Katsunan 94

labor, see industrial labor force; Japanese employment system; labor disputes
labor disputes 63–6, 69–72, 73–4, 114–18
land reform 136–7, 138, 144
land tax reform:
  (1873) 44–5
  (1991) 143–4
Liberal Democratic Party 124–6, 138, 162, 163
literacy, see education

London Naval Treaty 84–6

Matsukata deflation 49–50
Matsukata Masayoshi 48–9
Meiji Restoration, interpretations of 9, 12, 17–21
'middle-class' consciousness 127, 129
Miki Kiyoshi 98–9, 102
military (to 1945):
  constitutional provisions concerning 77–8
  and policy-making in the 1930s 77, 86–7
  politicization of the army and navy 81, 82–6
  popular attitudes toward 23, 65–6, 87–9
Minamata disease 120
Ministry of Agriculture, Forestry and Fisheries (MAFF) 138–9, 141, 143, 144
Ministry of Education 29–30, 65, 157–8
Ministry of International Trade and Industry (MITI) 111–12
Miyake Setsurei 94–5
monarchy, see emperor and imperial institution

national seclusion 11–12
navy, see military (to 1945)
Neo-Confucianism 15–17, 18–19
Nihonjinron (debate about Japaneseness) 99–103
'normal constitutional government', see party government (1918–32)

Occupation, American image of 105–6
oil crisis (1973) 108, 125–6

Pacific War, see Second World War

party government (1918–32) 76–7, 84, 88
population 41, 57
  age structure of 132–4

Rice Riots 55
right of supreme command 78, 85
Russo-Japanese War 26, 28, 32, 33, 55, 80, 83

Second World War:
  domestic impact of 104, 110, 162–3
  and Japanese intellectuals 99
  see also military (to 1945)
Shiga Shigetaka 93–4

Tanizaki Jun'ichirō 97
tenancy disputes 63–9, 71–3
Tōjō Hideki 77
Tokugawa shogunate 9–17
Tokutomi Sohō 93, 94, 95

urbanization 57–8, 59, 129–30

warrior class 9–10, 13–14, 15–21, 22–3, 44, 45, 50, 51–2
'welfare gap' 122–3, 125, 126
West, Japanese attitudes toward 19–21, 25–6, 34, 45, 91–5, 97–9, 100–3
women:
  aspirations of 55–6, 141–2, 147–9, 151–5
  education of 42, 151, 152, 157–8
  in labor force 42–3, 61, 117, 128, 132, 133–4, 149–51, 152–3, 154
  legal status of, under Meiji Civil Code 148–9
  lifetime birthrate of 132–3, 154

Yamagata Aritomo 79, 80
yamatodamashii (the Japanese spirit) 77, 83

MORE OXFORD PAPERBACKS

This book is just one of nearly 1000 Oxford Paperbacks currently in print. If you would like details of other Oxford Paperbacks, including titles in the World's Classics, Oxford Reference, Oxford Books, OPUS, Past Masters, Oxford Authors, and Oxford Shakespeare series, please write to:

UK and Europe: Oxford Paperbacks Publicity Manager, Arts and Reference Publicity Department, Oxford University Press, Walton Street, Oxford OX2 6DP.

Customers in UK and Europe will find Oxford Paperbacks available in all good bookshops. But in case of difficulty please send orders to the Cash-with-Order Department, Oxford University Press Distribution Services, Saxon Way West, Corby, Northants NN18 9ES. Tel: 01536 741519; Fax: 01536 746337. Please send a cheque for the total cost of the books, plus £1.75 postage and packing for orders under £20; £2.75 for orders over £20. Customers outside the UK should add 10% of the cost of the books for postage and packing.

USA: Oxford Paperbacks Marketing Manager, Oxford University Press, Inc., 200 Madison Avenue, New York, N.Y. 10016.

Canada: Trade Department, Oxford University Press, 70 Wynford Drive, Don Mills, Ontario M3C 1J9.

Australia: Trade Marketing Manager, Oxford University Press, G.P.O. Box 2784Y, Melbourne 3001, Victoria.

South Africa: Oxford University Press, P.O. Box 1141, Cape Town 8000.

POLITICS IN OXFORD PAPERBACKS
GOD SAVE ULSTER!
The Religion and Politics of Paisleyism
Steve Bruce

Ian Paisley is the only modern Western leader to have founded his own Church and political party, and his enduring popularity and success mirror the complicated issues which continue to plague Northern Ireland. This book is the first serious analysis of his religious and political careers and a unique insight into Unionist politics and religion in Northern Ireland today.

Since it was founded in 1951, the Free Presbyterian Church of Ulster has grown steadily; it now comprises some 14,000 members in fifty congregations in Ulster and ten branches overseas. The Democratic Unionist Party, formed in 1971, now speaks for about half of the Unionist voters in Northern Ireland, and the personal standing of the man who leads both these movements was confirmed in 1979 when Ian R. K. Paisley received more votes than any other member of the European Parliament. While not neglecting Paisley's 'charismatic' qualities, Steve Bruce argues that the key to his success has been his ability to embody and represent traditional evangelical Protestantism and traditional Ulster Unionism.

'original and profound . . . I cannot praise this book too highly.' Bernard Crick, *New Society*

HISTORY IN OXFORD PAPERBACKS
TUDOR ENGLAND
John Guy

Tudor England is a compelling account of political and religious developments from the advent of the Tudors in the 1460s to the death of Elizabeth I in 1603.

Following Henry VII's capture of the Crown at Bosworth in 1485, Tudor England witnessed far-reaching changes in government and the Reformation of the Church under Henry VIII, Edward VI, Mary, and Elizabeth; that story is enriched here with character studies of the monarchs and politicians that bring to life their personalities as well as their policies.

Authoritative, clearly argued, and crisply written, this comprehensive book will be indispensable to anyone interested in the Tudor Age.

'lucid, scholarly, remarkably accomplished . . . an excellent overview' *Sunday Times*

'the first comprehensive history of Tudor England for more than thirty years' Patrick Collinson, *Observer*

OPUS

*General Editors: Walter Bodmer,
Christopher Butler, Robert Evans,
John Skorupski*

CLASSICAL THOUGHT

Terence Irwin

Spanning over a thousand years from Homer to Saint Augustine, *Classical Thought* encompasses a vast range of material, in succinct style, while remaining clear and lucid even to those with no philosophical or Classical background.

The major philosophers and philosophical schools are examined—the Presocratics, Socrates, Plato, Aristotle, Stoicism, Epicureanism, Neoplatonism; but other important thinkers, such as Greek tragedians, historians, medical writers, and early Christian writers, are also discussed. The emphasis is naturally on questions of philosophical interest (although the literary and historical background to Classical philosophy is not ignored), and again the scope is broad—ethics, the theory of knowledge, philosophy of mind, philosophical theology. All this is presented in a fully integrated, highly readable text which covers many of the most important areas of ancient thought and in which stress is laid on the variety and continuity of philosophical thinking after Aristotle.